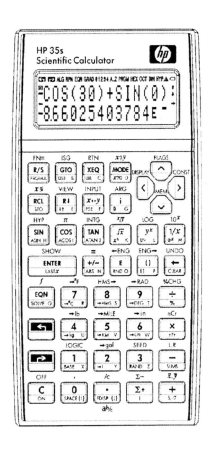

Surveying Solutions for the HP 35s Calculator

Manufactured in the United States of America

First printing December 2007
Second printing September 2008
Third printing July 2009
Fourth printing February 2010

published by **Software by** D'Zign
Tollhouse, California, U.S.A.

10 9 8 7 6 5

contents

description	text page	Program steps
program cautions and comments	1	
direction of a line	2	
Azimuth to Bearing	2	LBL A page 2
Bearing to Azimuth	3	LBL B page 3
add-subtract Degrees, minutes and seconds	4	LBL D page 4
vertical curves and grades	7	LBL V page 1P
station with elevation known	10	LBL E page 1P
vertical intersections	11	LBL H page 2P
circular curves	12	LBL C page 3P
circular curve layout	16	(2nd part C) 5P
triangle solutions	19	LBL G page 6P
coordinate geometry	26	
point storage and recall	26	LBL P page 9P
traverse	28	LBL T page 9P
traverse closure	30	LBL K page 10P
inversing used separately	32	LBL L page 11P
used during a traverse	34	LBL X page 34
for stakeout calculations	35	LBL S page 11P
intersections	36	LBL I page 11P
calculating missing sides	40	
line/curve to curve intersections	43	
slope staking as intersection	43	
trouble-shooting your programs	44	
answer key	44	
Maintenance (setting/clearing coordinate registers)	14P	LBL Z page 14P
Partially clearing Registers	14P	
program LN and checksum chart	**15P**	

Describing a book is usually easy . . . in this case it's a little more difficult because it isn't just one kind of book. The intent is for this manual to be an instruction manual on programming your HP35s calculator, a book of programs for the calculator, a review course on surveying and engineering calculations, and a workbook. It's also a Third Printing.

First, let's look at the calculator. What you have is the result of 35 years of development by Hewlett Packard in the field of scientific calculators.

The first HP35, in 1972, was an absolute engineering marvel to engineers and surveyors . . . it had the trigonometric functions built right in. Appendix G in your calculator's manual took 17½ pages just to list the programmable functions in the HP35s. You can (should) use Appendix G as a quick reference to the keystrokes used to access each function as you write your programs.

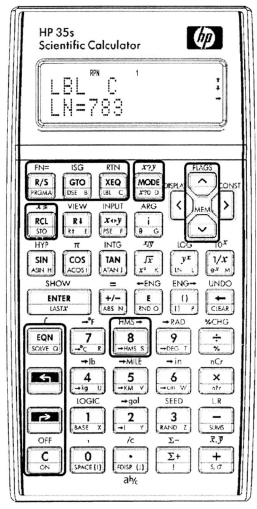

In the first row, the R/S key is used when you are running a program, or STOP as a program step; the *right-shifted* R/S is PRG, and it is what you press to go into program mode. The MODE key is most important for it's two shifted functions, x?y x?0. These have menus for inputting the tests for whether or not x's relationship to y or 0. There are 6 options for each. The use of RCL and STO should be obvious, as should be the shifted functions of the 8 key.

The *left-shifted* up-scroll key is FLAGS and has a menu for clearing, setting or testing various flags. The shift keys access the extended functions of another key, and the EQN key you will probably learn to hate.

Why? Because the calculator allows us to use user-defined prompts for input rather than just the built-in prompts, and these prompts require that you stroke the RCL key before each alpha letter you use in the prompt.

```
A001  LBL A      🔄 XEQ A
A002  SF 10      ⬅ ∧ 1 · 0
A003  AZIMUTH    EQN Then stroke RCL
                 before each alpha input
A004  HMS→       ⬅ 8
```

Let's start programming

Looking at the partial program (above right) all programs start with a LABEL. Step A003 is typical of a prompt, and it is input just like an equation. The difference is, with **flag 10 set** it will prompt and pause for input, if **flag 10 is clear** it will evaluate the equation or expression. The instruction is also typical of the way we write an equation or prompt instruction in our keystroke examples. The actual keystrokes, in this example, are:

EQN RCL A RCL Z RCL I RCL M RCL U RCL T RCL H and then ENTER to complete the step.

If a prompt requires a space as separator between words, the space key is the *right-shifted* 0 (zero) key. Numbers and symbols do not require stroking RCL before entering them in the equation.

We're going to pretty much walk you through putting in each of the programs in this book, but if you don't bother reading the User's Guide that came with your calculator past the "how to insert the batteries" and "turning the calculator on" parts, at **least look** through chapters 13 and 14 to get somewhat familiar with what we're doing here. The first program we want to input is the same one we gave you a glimpse of on page 1, Label A. It performs azimuth-to-bearing calculations for you.

input your first program-subroutine

This is the first program you will input, and it will be used both as a stand-alone program *and* as a subroutine to several other programs later. All of these programs work in **RPN and Degree mode**. Make sure that you are in the proper mode before beginning by stroking [MODE] [5] [MODE] [1]. Start at Program Top by stroking [GTO] [·] [·] and then [↱] [R/S], to input the program steps in the order shown. The step numbers and instructions should look like the ones shown.

In step A002, [↰] [^] takes you to the flags menu and [1] selects Set Flag. Stroking [·] will automatically insert a 1, and stroking [0] completes the line. Input for step A003 was explained on page 1.

In step A009, the ARG menu is accessed by stroking [↰] [TAN]. IP is the sixth item in the menu, but instead of scrolling down to select it, just stroke [6].

A001	LBL A	[↱] [XEQ] [A]
A002	SF 10	[↰] [^] [1] [·] [0]
A003	AZIMUTH	[EQN] *Then stroke* [RCL] *before each alpha input*
A004	HMS÷	[↰] [8]
A005	ENTER	[ENTER]
A006	ENTER	[ENTER]
A007	90	[9] [0]
A008	÷	[÷]
A009	IP	[↰] [TAN] [6]
A010	1	[1]
A011	+	[+]
A012	STO Q	[↱] [RCL] [Q]
A013	R↓	[R↓]
A014	ENTER	[ENTER]
A015	SIN	[SIN]
A016	ASIN	[↱] [SIN]
A017	ABS	[↱] [+/-]
A018	→HMS	[↱] [8]
A019	STO B	[↱] [RCL] [B]
A020	RCL Q	[RCL] [Q]
A021	RTN	[↰] [XEQ]

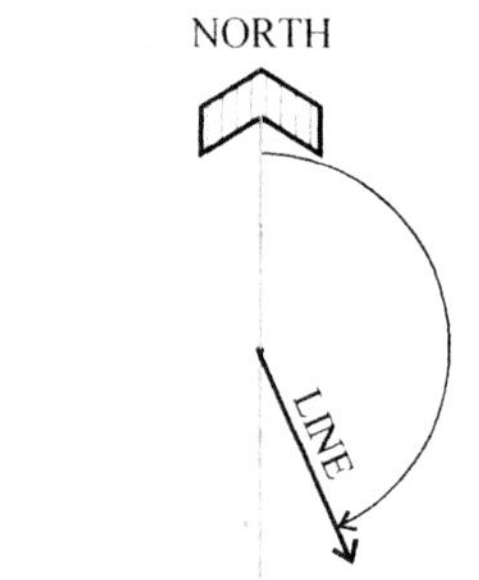

Directions by Azimuths

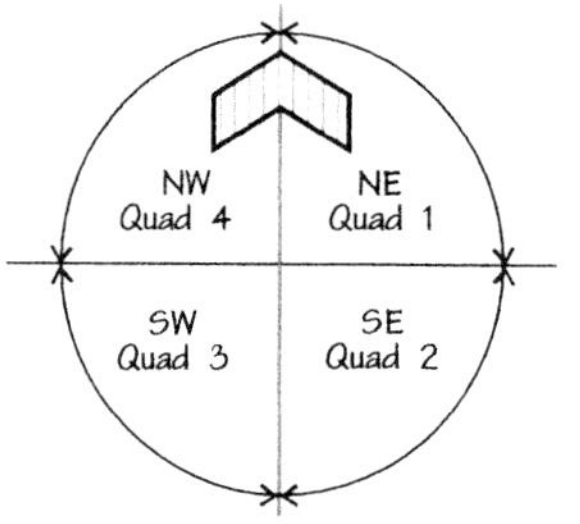

Directions by Bearings

In the U.S. azimuths are defined as the angle to the right from north, and range from 0° to 360° and bearings are defined by their quadrant, from 0° to 90°.

Angles are measured right (quad 1) or left (quad 4) of North when in quadrant 1 or 4, or right (quad 3) and left (quad 2) from 180° in 2 and 3. When an angle in quadrant 1 (NE) exceeds 90° it automatically becomes quadrant 2 and must be subtracted from 180° to be correct. **Mistakes happen more often in doing angle, or azimuth to bearing calculations than in any other type of calculation!**

PROGRAM: AZIMUTH TO BEARING/QUADRANT CODE

PROMPT	INSTRUCTIONS	KEYSTROKES	OUTPUT
		[XEQ] [A] [ENTER]	
AZIMUTH 0.0000	Input the Azimuth (D.ms)	[R/S]	BEARING (D.ms) QUAD CODE

ALL of the programs in this manual, use Degrees, Minutes and Seconds (DMS) for input and output. The second most common error in doing angle or bearing calculations is forgetting to change to or from degrees to decimal (or back) during keyboard calculations. We've reduced your chance of minor errors already, by taking out the need for this conversion.

With the program completed, try the example below.

EXAMPLE: CHANGE THE AZIMUTH, 125°23'16", TO BEARING AND QUADRANT CODE

PROMPT	INSTRUCTIONS	KEYSTROKES	OUTPUT
		[XEQ] [A] [ENTER]	
AZIMUTH	Input the Azimuth (D. ms)	[1][2][5][·][2][3][1][6][R/S]	54.3644 (D.ms) 2.0000

If it didn't give the correct answer there's something wrong with the program. You can do this with several examples and assume that the program is correctly input, or there is an easier (and more accurate) way to check the program steps.

Each program has a specific size, measured by it's length, and a checksum. **There is a complete chart on page 15P of the length (LN value) and checksum* (CK) to check your programs against.** The chart also indicates which registers and flags have been used within the program. Stroke [◄][▼] [2] to open the list of programs.

At this point you should see $\boxed{\begin{array}{l}\text{LBL A}\\\text{LN=73}\end{array}}$ stroke

[◄] and hold down [ENTER] to show $\boxed{\begin{array}{l}\text{CK=17B0}\\\text{LN=73}\end{array}}$

*In the earliest release of the HP35s calculators the checksums are not always the same in different calculators. For this book we will give the LN and checksum numbers, but you should **not** rely on the checksums to agree.

input your second program-subroutine

We've put in one program so far, and checked (or edited) it until it has the correct LN number, so this one should program faster. It has two prompts, the first for the bearing (has to be between 0° and 90°), the second for the quadrant code (see illustration on page 2).

Input the program. When you are finished, check it by stroking [◄][▼] [2] to open the list of programs, scroll to LBL B. You should have:

$\boxed{\begin{array}{l}\text{LBL B}\\\text{LN=95}\end{array}}$

If you got the right number, you're done, but you need to run some practice examples with it.

B001 LBL B	[►] [XEQ] [B]
B002 SF 10	[◄] [∧] [1][·][0]
B003 BEARING	[EQN] *Then stroke* [RCL] *before each alpha input*
B004 STO B	[►] [RCL] [B]
B005 QUAD CODE	[EQN] *Then stroke* [RCL] *before each alpha input*
B006 STO Q	[►] [RCL] [Q]
B007 x<>y	[x↔y]
B008 HMS→	[◄] [8]
B009 x<>y	[x↔y]
B010 ENTER	[ENTER]
B011 ENTER	[ENTER]
B012 2	[2]
B013 ÷	[÷]
B014 IP	[◄] [TAN] [6]
B015 π	[◄] [COS]
B016 →DEG	[►] [9]
B017 x	[×]
B018 x<>y	[x↔y]
B019 LASTx	[►] [ENTER]
B020 x	[×]
B021 COS	[COS]
B022 R↑	[►] [R↓]
B023 x	[×]
B024 -	[−]
B025 →HMS	[►] [8]
B026 RTN	[◄] [XEQ]

If you didn't get the right LN, the problem is in one of the steps. Check for an extra line or a missing line first. Stroke [GTO] [A] [ENTER], then enter program mode (stroke [🡒] [R/S]) and scroll through the program. You will be working on the program line that is in the X-register (the bottom one); it is an extra step and you can delete it by back-clearing it with the [←] key.

If you are missing a step, put the step that is supposed to be proceeding it in the X-register then type in the new step. When you're finished, do NOT forget to leave program mode by stroking [C], then try the program again.

PROGRAM: BEARING/QUADRANT CODE TO AZIMUTH

PROMPT	INSTRUCTIONS	KEYSTROKES	OUTPUT
		[XEQ] [B] [ENTER]	
BEARING	Input the Bearing (D.ms)	[R/S]	
QUAD CODE	Input the Quadrant Code	[R/S]	AZIMUTH (D.ms)

EXAMPLE: CHANGE THE BEARING, N 25°23'16" W, TO AN AZIMUTH		[XEQ] [B] [ENTER]	
PROMPT	INSTRUCTIONS	KEYSTROKES	OUTPUT
BEARING	Input the Bearing (D.ms)	[2] [5] [.] [2] [3] [1] [6] [R/S]	
QUAD CODE	Input the Quadrant Code	[4] [R/S]	334.3644

. You will have noted that the response to a prompt in this calculator does not require that you ENTER the input. You stroke the [R/S] key instead, to tell the program that input is complete and the program should continue.

While that example (above) answer is still in the X-register, try this; stroke [XEQ] [A] [0] [0] [4]. That should turn your last answer back into a bearing/quad. The HP35s calculator allows us to execute a particular program step anywhere in program memory as long as we know the *address* of that step. What we've just done is the same conversion you typed in as LBL A, but we have bypassed the prompt and it ran automatically. This is how it will be used as a sub-routine in later programs.

input your third program-subroutine
We'll add the short program (right) to our collection (it adds and subtracts in D.ms). This one is different from the first two. In those, you executed the programs and they prompted for input. In this one, you input the numbers first and then execute the program. There are no prompts

INSTRUCTIONS	KEYSTROKES	OUTPUT
Input the 1st angle or azimuth (D.ms)	[ENTER]	
Input the 2nd angle or azimuth (D.ms) (to subtract, first stroke [+/−])	[XEQ] [D] [ENTER]	DIFFERENCE OR SUM

D001 LBL D   [🡒] [XEQ] [D]
D002 x<>y   [x↔y]
D003 HMS→   [◁] [8]
D004 x<>y   [x↔y]
D005 HMS→   [◁] [8]
D006 x<>y   [x↔y]
D007 +   [+]
D008 →HMS   [🡒] [8]
D009 RTN   [◁] [XEQ]

Start at the top of program memory by stroking [GTO] [.] [.] and then [🡒] [R/S] to begin input. You should end up with LN=27, as shown in the chart on page 14P.

There are several ways to work this example, for instance you could change both bearings to azimuths and subtract them . . . but that is the angle from S 23°15'44" E to N 17°22'41" W, so you would have to subtract that answer from 360°. You could change the SE bearing to an azimuth and add the NW bearing angle to it.

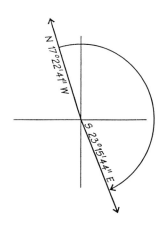

This is essentially what we do in the solution below, but rather than run the bearing/quad to azimuth program, we just subtract the bearing value from 180° and come out with the same result (with less keystrokes and a better chance to actually look at the problem before we complicate it).

EXAMPLE: WHAT IS THE ANGLE BETWEEN N 17°22'41" W AND S 23°15'44" E?	XEQ B ENTER	
INSTRUCTIONS	**KEYSTROKES**	**OUTPUT**
Get the angle between North and S 23°15'44" E	1 8 0 ENTER	
	2 3 . 1 5 4 4 +/− XEQ D ENTER	156.4416
Add the other angle	1 7 . 2 2 4 1 XEQ D ENTER	174.0657

Now we'll start on the 'workbook' part of this book. You're going to do part of the exercises either longhand or with the calculator, but you want to remember that the calculator functions for adding and subtracting work in decimal degrees, not D.ms, and pay attention to bringing them back to D.ms after the calculation as well as changing them before input. The same thing applies to the trigonometric functions.

To change D.ms to decimal stroke ◄ 8 to change decimal to D.ms stroke ► 8. When you use the programs, none of this is necessary because it's done for you and you only work in D.ms.

Exercise 1 *(do the first two longhand, then complete the exercise with the programs)*
The answer key for the exercises is in the back of the book, beginning on page 44

  1.   Add the angles, 28°15'34", 102°52'41", and 16°16'08" *ans:* _____

  2.   Subtract 28°15'34 from 102°52'41", then add 16°16'08" *ans:* _____

  3.   Add the angle, 102°52'41", to a bearing of N 62°45'23" W *ans:* _____

  4.   Subtract 98°15'59" from a bearing of N 01°14'17" E *ans:* _____

Exercise 2 (do #s 1, 2, 5 and 6 longhand, then complete the exercise with the programs) Calculate the angles indicated

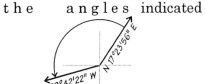 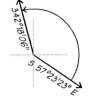 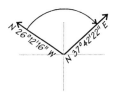 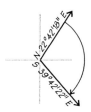

  1. *ans:* _____   2. *ans:* _____   3. *ans:* _____   4. *ans:* _____

Continued on the next page

Calculate the azimuth or bearing as indicated

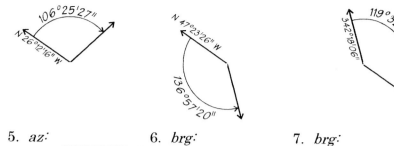

5. *az:* _____ 6. *brg:* _____ 7. *brg:* _____ 8. *az:* _____

What are the answers to the following

9. Cosine 17°15'23" _____ 10. Tangent 104°52'26" _____ 11. Sine 92°00'10" _____

12. Find the Sine of 197°14'23", then find the arcsine of the answer and change it back to D.ms.

editing a program

We're going to go back and edit the last program, LBL D, adding a subroutine to the bottom of it. This subroutine will be used in future programming to clear left-over garbage from previous programs.

On the calculator, stroke GTO D 0 0 9 and then ⤢ R/S to enter program mode. You should see:

Type in the new steps D010 through D026, using the keystrokes shown at the right. (note that we show the face value of the keys instead of the function. When you are done, exit program mode and check the LN number for LBL D. It should now be LN=80.

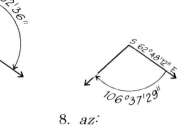

D009	RTN	
D010	CLVARS	⤢ ← 2
D011	CF 0	◁ ∧ 2 0
D012	CF 1	◁ ∧ 2 1
D013	CF 2	◁ ∧ 2 2
D014	CF 3	◁ ∧ 2 3
D015	FS? 4	◁ ∧ 3 4
D016	4	4
D017	STO X	⤢ RCL X
D018	CF 4	◁ ∧ 2 4
D019	x≠0?	⤢ MODE 1
D020	SF 4	◁ ∧ 1 4
D021	CF 5	◁ ∧ 2 5
D022	CF 6	◁ ∧ 2 6
D023	0	0
D024	STO X	⤢ RCL X
D025	CLSTK	⤢ ← 5
D026	RTN	◁ XEQ

What did I just do? Because we can address a subroutine directly, by address, we have just added a subroutine that can be used at the start of some new programs from now on, instead of each program having to start with essentially the flag/stack/vars clearing routine. Steps D015 through D020 are required because one of the programs we are going to input later uses Flag 04 to signal that it is to retain data. **And**, you've just learned how to edit a program.

On the next few pages we are going to look at some various vertical curve solutions. We'll also write the programs that make them work. **The program pages start with Page 1P, located at the back of the book, after page 46.** They are printed in a non-reproducible blue ink in an effort to help protect our copyright on the programs in this book. After you've read pages 8 and 9, start typing in the steps for LBL V on page P1.

vertical curves and grades

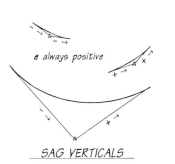

CREST VERTICALS

SAG VERTICALS

Vertical curves are usually described as 'crest' or 'sag' verticals, as shown to the left.

The form of the curve may be expressed as

$$y = ax^2 + bx$$

where y is the height of the curve above or below the first tangent point, and x is the distance therefrom.

The **highest** or **lowest** point on the curve is at a point where the gradient of the tangent is equal to **0%**. This is called the "turning point" of the curve. If both gradients have the same sign, there is no actual turning point, and the vertical direction is continuous. The gradient of the tangent may be found by differentiating y with respect to x in the equation above.

When

$$dy/dx = 0, \quad x = -b/2a.$$

Our program for vertical curves is designed to do quick vertical curve and grade calculations. The number of entries you make during input tells the program whether you are calculating a grade or a curve.

Formulas for vertical curves and grades vary with the known values when you begin to solve the grade or curve. In most vertical curve cases, if you are working from a set of plans, you would know the beginning station (BVC) and it's elevation, the ending station (EVC) and it's elevation, the length and the grade in (Gi) and the grade out (Go). In most cases, the intersection point (PVI) is given too. The following would apply:

If the high or low point elevation and the beginning station (EL$_0$ and PVC) are known,

1. $$\left(\frac{Go - Gi}{200L}\right)(STA - BVC)^2 + \left(\frac{Gi}{100}\right)(STA - BVC) + (El_{bvc} - El_{sta}) = 0 \quad (ax^2 + bx + c = 0)$$

If the high or low point elevation and the intersection station (EL$_0$ and PVI) are known,

2. $$L = 200(El_{bvc} - El_0)(Go - Gi)\left(\frac{1}{Gi^2}\right)$$

3. $$L = 200(El_{bvc} - El_0)(Go - Gi)\left(\frac{1}{GoGi}\right)$$

Where:
Gi = Beginning grade (grade in), expressed in percent
Go = Ending grade (grade out), expressed in percent
L = Length of curve, measured in along the horizontal
STA = Station along horizontal with curve elevation
El_{sta} = elevation at STA
BVC = Beginning station (point of curve)

El_{bvc} = Beginning elevation at BVC
PVI = Point of tangent intersection
El_{pvi} = Elevation at the PVI
EL_0 = Elevation at high or Low point of curve
EVC = Ending station (end of curve)
El_{evc} = Elevation at the EVC

There is a question that often occurs in tests, but is never used in the real world; Given the High/Low point elevation, the grades in and out, and either the PVI elevation or the BVC elevation and want to know the minimum length of curve that will work. Minimum lengths are NEVER used, and the difference in grades is used to select the required length from a table that takes passing sight distance into consideration.

If the PVI is given

$$L = 200(EL_{pvi} - EL_0)(G_0 - G_i)\left(\frac{1}{G_i^2}\right)$$

or, if the BVC is given.

$$L = 200(EL_{bvc} - EL_0)(G_0 - G_i)\left(\frac{1}{G_0 G_i}\right)$$

We've not included a program that will do this type of problem but do suggest that the above formulas can be input as equations in the equation library in case you need them. rather than include a program for this one case, we programmed for the day to day vertical calculations that you are more likely to encounter.

PROGRAM: CALCULATING ALONG A VERTICAL TANGENT OR CURVE

PROMPT	INSTRUCTIONS	KEYSTROKES	OUTPUT
		[XEQ] [V] [ENTER]	
BEG STA	Input the station at the B.V.C.	[R/S]	
BEG ELEV	Input the elevation at the B.V.C.	[R/S]	
GRADE IN	Input the % of grade for the tangent. (For a curve, input the % of grade for the incoming grade) Change sign if negative	[R/S]	
GRADE OUT	**No input for a vertical tangent.** For a curve, input the % of grade for the outgoing grade) Change sign if negative	[R/S]	
LENGTH	**No input for a vertical tangent.** (For a curve, input the length of the vertical curve)	[R/S]	
	When calculating along a vertical curve, the turning point station and elevation are automatically output at this point. Stroke [R/S] to continue		STATION @ 0% ELEVATION @ 0%
INPUT STA	Input the next station you want to calculate the elevation for	[R/S]	STATION ELEVATION
	After writing down the answers, stroke [R/S] to continue with the next station	[R/S]	
INPUT STA	When finished with the calculations	[C]	

EXAMPLE

The vertical curve shown to the right will be used for the example. The B.V.C. station is 10+50, at elevation 106.00.

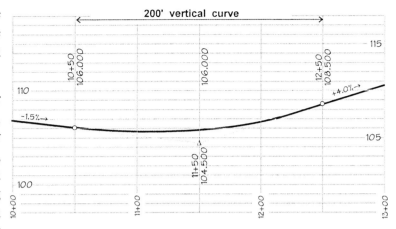

We will calculate the elevations for stations at 50 foot intervals along the curve, the 0% station and elevation (high/low point), in this example the low point. Later, you will also be able to calculate the station at which a particular elevation occurs, using [LBL] [E] [ENTER], after all of the information has been entered for the vertical tangent or curve you are working on.

PROGRAM EXAMPLE: CALCULATING ALONG A VERTICAL TANGENT OR CURVE

PROMPT	INSTRUCTIONS	KEYSTROKES	OUTPUT
		[XEQ] [V] [ENTER]	
BEG STA	Input the station at the B.V.C.	[1][0][5][0] [R/S]	
BEG ELEV	Input the elevation at the B.V.C.	[1][0][6] [R/S]	
GRADE IN	Input the % of grade for the incoming grade. (Change sign if negative)	[1][.][5] [+/−] [R/S]	
GRADE OUT	Input the % of grade for the outgoing grade Change sign if negative	[4] [R/S]	
LENGTH	Input the length of the vertical curve. **Output is high/low point sta & elev**	[2][0][0] [R/S]	1104.5455 105.5909
		[R/S]	
INPUT STA	Input the next station	[1][1][0][0] [R/S]	1100.0000 105.5938
		[R/S]	
INPUT STA	Input the next station	[1][1][5][0] [R/S]	1150.000 105.8750
		[R/S]	
INPUT STA	Input the next station	[1][2][0][0] [R/S]	1200.000 106.8438
		[R/S]	
INPUT STA	Input the next station	[1][2][5][0] [R/S]	1250.000 108.5000
		[C]	

NOTE: Because the calculator does not use menus, as the graphic calculators do, we use a sort of *vertical* menu. You Run/Stop through all of the possible prompts, only inputting data where you know it.

Once you have finished with the vertical curves and grades program, and have checked (and run) it, we'll put in this next one. It is LBL E, and the program steps begin on page 1P. With this one you can specify an elevation and it will calculate the station where that station occurs. Actually, it calculates two stations . . . only one of them will be within the curve you're working on, but it's easy to tell which one to use. It's also a good idea to run that station, by station, when you've returned to the curve.

When you press [R/S] after the calculation from this program the high/low information will be shown. Stroke [R/S] again for the INPUT STA prompt. The example below assumes you are still in the vertical curve in the last example.

PROGRAM: CALCULATE STATION WHEN ELEVATION IS KNOWN

PROMPT	INSTRUCTIONS	KEYSTROKES	OUTPUT
None . . .	Input the elevation (two stations will be shown, verify that they are within the curve to be valid answers.	[XEQ] [E] [ENTER]	STATION STATION
	Next output is the high/low point	[R/S]	STATION ELEVATION
	Return to original program	[R/S]	
INPUT STA			

EXAMPLE: FIND THE STATION AT WHICH ELEVATION 105.65 OCCURS		[1][0][5][·][6][5] [XEQ] [E] [ENTER]	
	Output is the station(s) at which the elevation occurs.		1125.2800 1083.8100
		[R/S]	
	Output is the high/low point		1104.5455 105.5909
		[R/S]	
INPUT STA	Continue with input in main program		

Exercise 3

Calculate the indicated stations for a 300 foot vertical curve with a PVI at station 15+00, if the grade in is 2% and the grade out is –3% The elevation at the PVI is 102.75.

1. BVC station _____ elevation _____ high point station _____ elevation _____

EVC station _____ elevation _____

2. Calculate the elevations for the following stations:

14+20 _____ 14+50 _____ 15+22 _____ 15+50 _____ 16+10 _____

3.   At what station will the elevation 100.58 occur? _____ & _____

There are also times when you have known stations and elevations along two vertical tangents and need to calculate the point of intersection between them. This program will calculate the intersection point when the grades, any starting point, and any ending point are known.

Once the point of intersection (P.V.I.) is known, a curve length may be selected and a B.V.C. station and elevation calculated. From there, use the vertical program to calculate the stations along the curve.

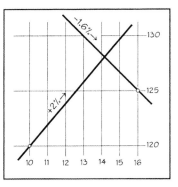

The example will use the information from the illustration to the right. The known station at the beginning is 10+00, with an elevation of 120.00 and the known station at the end is 16+00 at elevation 125.00.

The two known grades are a +2.00 percent and a minus 1.60 percent. Follow the procedure below to obtain the station and elevation of the point of intersection.

PROGRAM: CALCULATE VERTICAL INTERSECTION

PROMPT	INSTRUCTIONS	KEYSTROKES	OUTPUT
		XEQ H ENTER	
STA 1	Input the first station	R/S	
ELEV 1	Input the elevation	R/S	
STA 2	Input the second station	R/S	
ELEV 2	Input the elevation	R/S	
GRADE IN	Input the % of grade for the grade in. (Change sign if negative)	R/S	
GRADE OUT	Input the % of grade for the grade out (Change sign if negative)	R/S	PVI STATION ELEVATION

EXAMPLE: FIND THE STATION AND ELEVATION OF THE VERTICAL INTERSECTION

PROMPT	INSTRUCTIONS	KEYSTROKES	OUTPUT
		XEQ H ENTER	
STA 1	Input the first station	1 0 0 0 R/S	
ELEV 1	Input the elevation	1 2 0 R/S	
STA 2	Input the second station	1 6 0 0 R/S	
ELEV 2	Input the elevation	1 2 5 R/S	
GRADE IN	Input the % of grade for the grade in (Change sign if negative)	2 R/S	
GRADE OUT	Input the % of grade for the grade out (Change sign if negative)	1 . 6 +/− R/S	1405.5556 128.1111

Exercise 4:

1.   Using the information from the example on the preceding page, calculate a 400' vertical curve to be used to round the grade along the roadway. Calculate the following:

BVC station _____ elevation _____ high point station _____

EVC station _____ elevation _____ high point elevation _____

2.   Calculate the elevations for the following stations:

12+00 _____   12+50 _____   13+00 _____   13+50 _____   14+00 _____

14+50 _____   15+00 _____   15+50 _____   16+00 _____

3.   At what stations will the elevations 123.58 and 121.56 occur? _____ & _____

circular curves

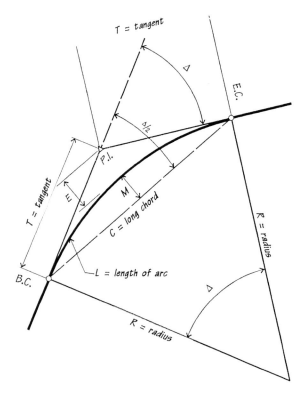

Curve Nomenclature
The parts of a typical horizontal (circular) curve are shown above

You are probably very familiar with circular curves, but to better understand what these programs do, we'll review the definitions, symbols used, and the formulas for calculating the different parts.

PI, Point of Intersection is the point where the two tangents intersect.

Central Angle, commonly called Delta (Δ) or I, it is the deflection angle measured, at the point of intersection, between the back and forward tangents. Most often this is one of the known parts essential to the calculation of other parts of the curve.

Deflection angle (ϕ), what we call the deflection angle is one-half the central angle, or the angle, turned at the BC of the curve, from the PI to the EC. There is also an angle from the BC to any point on the curve that is called the deflection angle when calculating stations for stakeout.

Length of curve (L), is the distance between the beginning and end of the curve measured along the curve. Arc Length.

$$L = 100\Delta R(\pi/180°)$$

Tangent Distance (T), actually a "semi-tangent" to the curve, it is the distance between the PI and the beginning or end of the curve and the two tangents are always equal.

$$T = R\tan\Delta/2$$

Radius (R), the "radius" is normally referred to by its length.

Long Chord (LC), the long chord is the distance between the beginning and end of the curve points of tangency, and is the length for angle Δ.

$$LC = 2Rsin\Delta/2$$

Chord (C), Also called the 'chord', or 'short chord' is the distance from the BC of the curve to any point on the curve, for angle ϕ.

$$C = 2Rsin\phi/2$$

BC (or PC), the 'beginning of curve' or 'point of curvature' both common usage in different parts of the U.S.

EC (or PT) the 'end of curve' or 'point of tangency' both common usage in different parts of the U.S.

Middle Ordinate (M), length of ordinate from the middle of the long chord to the middle of the curve.

$$M = R(1-cos\Delta/2) = Rvers\Delta/2$$

External (E), distance from PI to the middle of the curve.

$$E = R(sec\Delta/2-1) = Rexsec\Delta/2$$

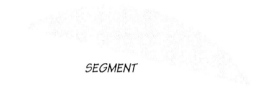

SEGMENT

SECTOR

FILLET

Curve Area Nomenclature

The three common measurements for areas of a typical horizontal (circular) curve are shown above

Segment area, the area between the arc of the curve and the long chord of the curve.

$$Segment\ area = Sector\ area - \tfrac{1}{2}R^2sin\Delta$$
$$= Sector\ area - \tfrac{1}{2}CRcos(\Delta/2)$$

Sector area, the 'pie-shaped' area – from the radius point to the B.C., along the arc of the curve to the E.C. and back to the radius point.

$$Sector\ area = \pi R^2\Delta/360 = LR/2$$

Fillet area, the area between the tangents of the curve and the arc of the curve. Often used for calculating pavement areas at the returns on street intersections.

$$Fillet\ area = RT - Sector\ area$$

The Circular Curve program . . . The program for circular curve solutions, LBL C, begins on page **3P** and is a long one. It uses a series of prompts that let you decide what known parts you have as you R/S through them.

We will also take advantage of the INPUT and PSE functions for the first time, and complete part of the program (and work with it) before going back to edit and expand it. Some of the expression (equation) input is longer than our column format will permit on just one line, but **should be typed in as one line.**

This program is one that requires flexibility in input, and the HP35s doesn't include any functions for creating a user-defined menu. The program requires input of any two of five different options, so we've again created a sort of 'vertical' menu. Remember that you Run/Stop through *all* of the options.

You can solve a curve if you know the **Delta** Angle or **Radius** and any one of these parameters; Length, Chord or Tangent. As you [R/S] through the prompts each option is presented (in the order above) for consideration. If for instance, you don't know the Delta value you stroke [R/S] without any input. If you are prompted for one of the parameters that is known, input the value and *then* stroke [R/S]. You *must respond to all of the prompts*, one way or the other, until the end of the group and the program. The calculation then begins automatically.

Another new type of selection menu used in this program allows you to branch . . . to either of two options. The prompt, MORE=0 STAKE=1, will either take you back to the top of the program for calculation of a new curve or branch you to a sub-routine that lets you stake out the curve. To choose, input either 0 or 1 and stroke [R/S].

For now, we'll program steps C001 through C189. This includes the prompt portion, but not the programming for the stakeout sub-routine, we'll test and run the curve program first and complete the other routine later.

PROGRAM: CIRCULAR CURVES

	PROMPT	INSTRUCTIONS	KEYSTROKES	OUTPUT
1		Begin the program	[XEQ] [C] [ENTER]	
2	DELTA	If the CENTRAL ANGLE is known, input it (D.ms format), if not known, no input **Either the central angle or radius *must* be input as one of the known parts**	[R/S]	
3	R?	If the RADIUS is known, input it, otherwise no input **Either the central angle or radius *must* be input as one of the known parts**	[R/S]	
4	L?	If known, input the length of arc, otherwise no input	[R/S]	
5	C?	If known, input the chord distance otherwise no input	[R/S]	
6	T?	If known, input the tangent distance otherwise no input	[R/S]	I = Central Angle
7				R = Radius
8			[R/S]	L = Arc Length
9			[R/S]	C = Chord Distance
10			[R/S]	

Continued on next page

11			R/S	T = Tangent Distance
12			R/S	E = External Distance
13			R/S	M = Mid-Ordinate Distance
14		AREAS reminder displayed for 1 second	R/S	
15		SECTOR reminder (1 second prompt)	R/S	SECTOR AREA
16		SEGMENT reminder (1 second prompt)	R/S	SEGMENT AREA
17		FILLET reminder (1 second prompt)	R/S	FILLET AREA
18	MORE=0 STAKE=1	To calculate another curve, input 0, **or** to calculate stakeout for this curve input 1 **Or**, to leave the program stroke C	R/S	

Exercise 5:

Complete the curve data for the following:

1.
Radius =   510.23'

Delta =

Length =

Tangent =

Chord =   244.77'

External =

Mid-Ordinate =

2.
Radius =   400.00'

Delta =

Length =

Tangent =   125.16'

Chord =

External =

Mid-Ordinate =

Sector =

Segment =

Fillet =

3.
Radius =   200.00'

Delta =

Length =   10.26'

Tangent =

Chord =

External =

Mid-Ordinate =

Sector =

Segment =

Fillet =

4.
Radius =

Delta =   1°25'16"

Length =

Tangent =

Chord =   400.00'

External =

Mid-Ordinate =

Circular Curve Layout

The most common method for staking out a curve is the deflection-offset method, using chord solutions to each of the station intervals to be staked.

Once a curve has been calculated using the circular curve program, you can continue into the layout program to calculate the chord and deflection angles to any stations to be set.

The layout program also calculates solutions for layout by the tangent-offset and chord-offset methods, and includes an option to stake the curve at an offset to the centerline instead of on the centerline itself. Offsets to the curve on the outside are input as positive, if the offset is to the inside of the curve, input the offset as negative.

Initial prompts are for selection of the type of output you want. Input a number for the type you want, and just stroke R/S for the others. This will be followed by a prompt for the offset, if any. To just calculate centerline stroke R/S or input the width of the offset and stroke R/S. The program will prompt for station and then output the stakeout information. You can run the program again to generate a different type, or input another curve and generate the stakeout information for it.

Return to page 5P and, on the calculator, stroke GTO C 1 8 9 and then 🔁 R/S. Complete the input of program LBL C.

deflection and long chord
With the instrument at the B.C. of the curve, the deflection angle is turned as the angle from the P.I. The long chord is the distance from the B.C. to the station being set.

chord/offset method
Similar to the tangent/offset method, except that the distance is pulled along the full chord of the curve to a point opposite the station being set. Often used on curves in tunnels with the laser line set on the long chord.

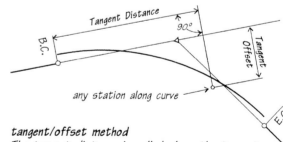

tangent/offset method
The tangent distance is pulled along the tangent line (semi-tangent of the curve), and a temporary point is set. The offset distance is measured to the station being set, at right angles to the tangent.

The instructions on the next page start at a point after the use of the circular curve program, which calculates the curve. On the pages following we address the layout of the circular curves (having already stored the required data about the curve), giving the user these three methods of stakeout to chose from.

The selection menu used in this program lets you [R/S] through the prompts for the types of output you don't want and, by typing in a 1 (or any number) before [R/S] pick the one you do want. This selection will tell the program which type of output you want. At the very start of the program the "SELECT TYPE" reminder will pop up and then go away after being displayed for one second . . . similar to the reminder for "AREAS" in the previous program.

PROGRAM: CIRCULAR CURVE LAYOUT

	PROMPT	INSTRUCTIONS	KEYSTROKES	OUTPUT
1		After calculation of the curve, begin the curve layout program by responding [1] to the final prompt in the curve program		
2	SELECT TYPE	Reminder prompt will be displayed for one second		
3	DEFLECTION	To select this option, input any number and stroke [R/S] **OR** to not use this type, just stroke [R/S] without input		
4	TAN-OS	To select this option, input any number and stroke [R/S] **OR** to not use this type, just stroke [R/S] without input		
5	CHD-OS	To select this option, input any number and stroke [R/S] **OR** to not use this type, just stroke [R/S] without input		
6	OFFSET=	To calculate the layout at an offset, input the size of the offset (change sign for offsets to the inside of the curve). For calculations along centerline, just stroke [R/S] without input	[R/S]	
7	BC STATION	Input the station of the B.C.	[R/S]	
8	INPUT STA	Input the station you want to calculate layout for. Output is selection dependent	[R/S]	
9	DEF ANGLE TAN DIST or CHD DIST	Selection dependent prompt	[R/S]	
				VALUE
			[R/S]	
10	CHORD or OFFSET	Selection dependent prompt	[R/S]	
11				VALUE
12			[R/S]	
	INPUT STA	Returns you to step 8. Input the next station you want to calculate and repeat steps 8 through 12, or stroke [C] to leave the layout program		

Exercise 6:

Complete the curve data for the following, and then calculate the layout information for the stations as indicated:

1. Layout by deflection and chord

		STATION	DEFLECTION	CHORD
Radius =	510.23'	12+19.23 B.C.		
Delta =		12+50		
Length =		13+00		
Tangent =		13+50		
Chord =	244.77'	14+00		
External =		14+50		
Mid-Ordinate =		E.C.		

2. Layout by tangent-offset

		STATION	TANGENT DIST.	OFFSET
Radius =	400.00'	122+34.97 B.C.		
Delta =		122+50		
Length =		123+00		
Tangent =	125.16'	123+50		
Chord =		124+00		
External =		124+50		
Mid-Ordinate =		E.C.		

3. Layout by chord-offset

		STATION	CHORD DIST.	OFFSET
Radius =		53+24.37 B.C.		
Delta =	35°15'22"	53+50		
Length =	237.71'	54+00		
Tangent =		54+50		
Chord =		55+00		
External =		55+50		
Mid-Ordinate =		E.C.		

triangle solutions

The triangle shown to the right will be used for the examples. It should be noted that the output will vary slightly, depending on the number of places input, particularly in the input of the angles.

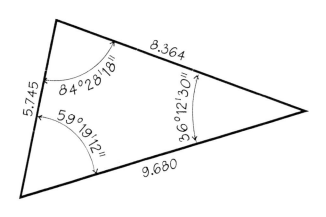

The notations for angles and sides is familiar to HP users, but is not the standard, or *textbook* notation which you will have learned in trigonometry (side **a** opposite angle **A**, side **b** opposite angle **B**, and side **c** opposite angle **C**). The sides and angles are numbered, in order, going around the triangle as shown below.

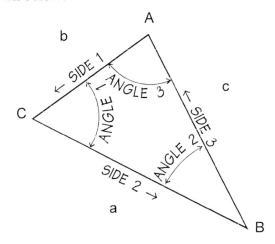

In the example shown below, the assigned designations go clockwise, if it will better fit the information available, the labeling may go counter-clockwise instead, as shown to the left.

Remember, side 1 is wherever you put it.

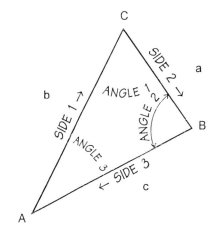

The example triangle (above) shows this style of labeling, compared to the standard notation for sides and angles.

Side 1 may be assigned to any side that is convenient to use, depending upon the available information about the triangle. It should be located at a side where the known information then falls into position for solution by one of the routines.

The program begins with selection prompts for you to select the TYPE of solution needed. A brief reminder prompt, TYPE SELECTION, is displayed (one second) and then the 5 type options are offered. To *NOT* select one of the types just stroke R/S. To select one, input 1 (or any number).

Continue with R/S through any remaining TYPE SELECTION options until you get the first of the three input prompts. Which of the prompts you get will depend on the TYPE, and will be in the same order as that specific type calls for. The instructions are on the next page, and the program steps (LBL G) begin on page 6P.

PROGRAM: TRIANGLE SOLUTIONS

	PROMPT	INSTRUCTIONS	KEYSTROKES	OUTPUT
1		Begin the program	[XEQ] [G] [ENTER]	
2	TYPE SELECTION	APPEARS BRIEFLY AS A REMINDER		
3	S1-S2-S3	SOLUTION FOR THREE SIDES KNOWN	Input a number to select this option or [R/S] to continue to next prompt	
4	A3-S1-A1	SOLUTION FOR TWO ANGLES AND THE INCLUDED SIDE KNOWN	Input a number to select this option or [R/S] to continue to next prompt	
5	S1-A1-A2	KNOWN SIDE AND THE NEXT TWO FOLLOWING ANGLES KNOWN	Input a number to select this option or [R/S] to continue to next prompt	
6	S1-A1-S2	SOLUTION WHEN TWO SIDES AND THE INCLUDED ANGLE ARE KNOWN	Input a number to select this option or [R/S] to continue to next prompt	
7	S1-S2-A2	TWO SIDES AND THE FOLLOWING AN-GLE ARE KNOWN	Input a number to select this option or [R/S] to continue to next prompt	
8		Three input prompts will be shown. Input the value requested	[R/S] after each input	
9				SIDE 1
10			[R/S]	ANGLE 1
11			[R/S]	SIDE 2
12			[R/S]	ANGLE 2
13			[R/S]	SIDE 3
14			[R/S]	ANGLE 3
15			[R/S]	AREA
16	2ND SOLUTION	Appears when there is a second solution to the S1-S2-A2 type. The program will again repeat steps 9 through 15 but the **output will not be in the same order as the original input**	[R/S]	
17		When finished with the calculations, it will return you to the triangle program for next calculation, beginning at step 2	[R/S]	

Examples are shown on the following pages for each of the solution types individually, covering the prompt, input and output in each case.

	PROMPT	KEYSTROKES	OUTPUT
8a	INPUT SIDE 1	8 · 3 6 4 R/S	
8b	INPUT SIDE 2	9 · 6 8 R/S	
8c	INPUT SIDE 3	5 · 7 4 5 R/S	
9			SIDE 1
		R/S	8.3640
10		R/S	ANGLE 1
		R/S	36.1232
11		R/S	SIDE 2
		R/S	9.6800
12		R/S	ANGLE 2
		R/S	59.1912
13		R/S	SIDE 3
		R/S	5.7450
14		R/S	ANGLE 3
		R/S	84.2816
15		R/S	AREA
		R/S	23.9138

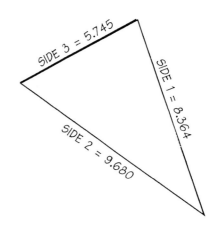

side 1, side 2, side 3

THREE SIDES KNOWN is one of the most used solutions for triangles, particularly since the accuracy of electronic distance measurement trilateration has, for the most part, replaced triangulation in several types of surveys. The example begins at the input prompts.

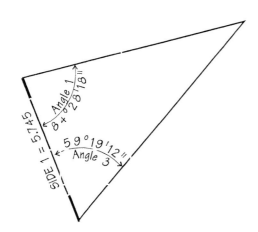

angle 3, side 1, angle 1

TWO ANGLES AND THE INCLUDED SIDE ARE KNOWN This solution is also used as a secondary solution to some of the other routines, after the problem has first been reduced to these three known parts.

	PROMPT	KEYSTROKES	OUTPUT
8a	INPUT ANGLE 3	5 9 · 1 9 1 2 R/S	
8b	INPUT SIDE 1	5 · 7 4 5 R/S	
8c	INPUT ANGLE 1	8 4 · 2 8 1 8 R/S	
9			SIDE 1
		R/S	5.7450
10		R/S	ANGLE 1
		R/S	84.2818
11		R/S	SIDE 2
		R/S	8.3641
12		R/S	ANGLE 2
		R/S	36.1230
13		R/S	SIDE 3
		R/S	9.6801
14		R/S	ANGLE 3
		R/S	59.1912
15		R/S	AREA
		R/S	23.9142

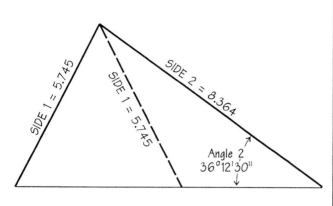

	PROMPT	KEYSTROKES	OUTPUT
8a	INPUT SIDE 1	5 . 7 4 5 R/S	
8b	INPUT SIDE 2	8 . 3 6 4 R/S	
8c	INPUT ANGLE 2	3 6 . 1 2 3 R/S	
9			SIDE 1
		R/S	5.7450
10		R/S	ANGLE 1
		R/S	84.2823
11		R/S	SIDE 2
		R/S	8.3640
12		R/S	ANGLE 2
		R/S	36.1230
13		R/S	SIDE 3
		R/S	9.6802
14		R/S	ANGLE 3
		R/S	59.1907
15		R/S	AREA
		R/S	23.9139
	2ND SOLUTION	R/S (output will continue with the second solution option)	
16			SIDE 1
		R/S	8.3640
17		R/S	ANGLE 1
		R/S	36.1230
18		R/S	SIDE 2
		R/S	3.8172
19		R/S	ANGLE 2
		R/S	120.4053
20		R/S	SIDE 3
		R/S	5.745
21		R/S	ANGLE 3
		R/S	23.0637
22		R/S	AREA
		R/S	9.4301

Note that the output is not in the same order as the original input.

side 1, side 2, angle 2

TWO SIDES AND THE FOLLOWING ANGLE KNOWN has two possible solutions. When this configuration is used, both solutions may be output. The second solution will not necessarily show the parts in the same order as the input.

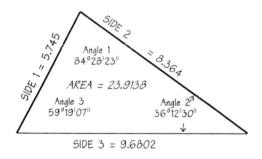

First Solution Output

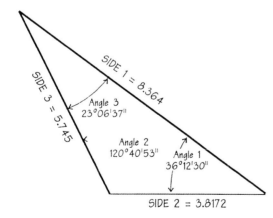

Second Solution Output

	PROMPT	KEYSTROKES	OUTPUT
8a	INPUT SIDE 1	5 . 7 4 5 R/S	
8b	INPUT ANGLE 1	8 4 . 2 8 1 8 R/S	
8c	INPUT SIDE 2	8 . 3 6 4 R/S	
9			SIDE 1
		R/S	5.740
10		R/S	ANGLE 1
		R/S	84.2818
11		R/S	SIDE 2
		R/S	8.3640
12		R/S	ANGLE 2
		R/S	36.1231
13		R/S	SIDE 3
		R/S	9.6800
14		R/S	ANGLE 3
		R/S	59.1911
15		R/S	AREA
		R/S	23.9138

side 1, angle 1, side 2

TWO SIDES AND THE INCLUDED ANGLE KNOWN is resolved by finding the third side, and then solving the triangle as shown on the previous page, three sides known.

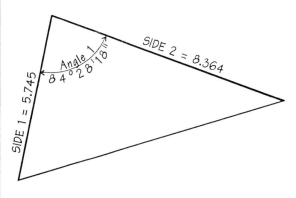

side 1, angle 1, angle 2

ONE SIDE AND THE TWO FOLLOWING ANGLES KNOWN This solution first solves for the third angle. The remainder of the triangle is solved as Angle, Side, Angle to determine the other missing sides.

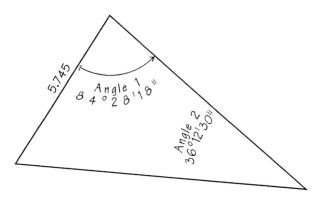

	PROMPT	KEYSTROKES	OUTPUT
8a	INPUT SIDE 1	5 . 7 4 5 R/S	
8b	INPUT ANGLE 1	8 4 . 2 8 1 8 R/S	
8c	INPUT ANGLE 2	3 6 . 1 2 3 R/S	
9			SIDE 1
		R/S	5.7450
10		R/S	ANGLE 1
		R/S	84.2818
11		R/S	SIDE 2
		R/S	8.3641
12		R/S	ANGLE 2
		R/S	36.1230
13		R/S	SIDE 3
		R/S	9.6801
14		R/S	ANGLE 3
		R/S	59.1912
15		R/S	AREA
		R/S	23.9142

Exercise 7:

1.   Solve the triangle

Side 1   _____

Angle 1   _____

Side 2   _____

Angle 2   _____

Side 3   _____

Angle 3   _____

Area   _____

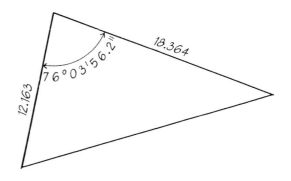

2.   Solve the triangle

Side 1   _____

Angle 1   _____

Side 2   _____

Angle 2   _____

Side 3   _____

Angle 3   _____

Area   _____

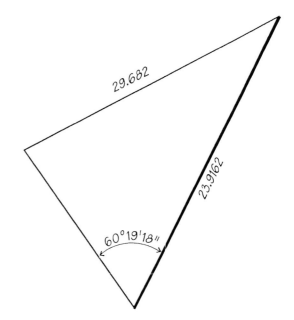

3.   Solve the triangle

Side 1   _____

Angle 1   _____

Side 2   _____

Angle 2   _____

Side 3   _____

Angle 3   _____

Area   _____

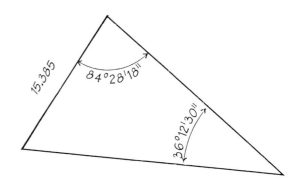

4.   Solve the triangle

Side 1   _____

Angle 1   _____

Side 2   _____

Angle 2   _____

Side 3   _____

Angle 3   _____

Area   _____

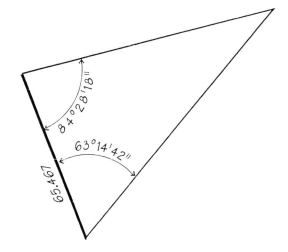

52.   Solve the triangle

Side 1   _____

Angle 1   _____

Side 2   _____

Angle 2   _____

Side 3   _____

Angle 3   _____

Area   _____

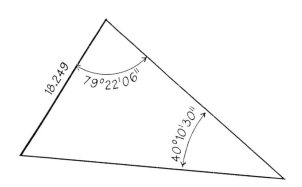

6.   Solve the triangle

Side 1   _____

Angle 1   _____

Side 2   _____

Angle 2   _____

Side 3   _____

Angle 3   _____

Area   _____

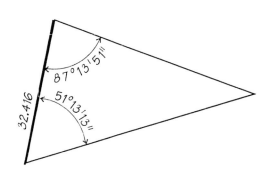

coordinate geometry

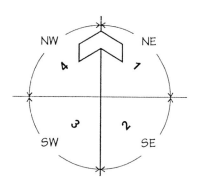

The backbone of Coordinate Geometry calculations is the relationship between coordinates with known values. If the coordinates for one point are known the direction and distance to a second point allows calculation of the new points coordinates, or if both points are known, we can calculate the direction and distance between them.

Bearings are input with quadrant codes and the quadrants are numbered with the same system that has been used by Hewlett-Packard since the first surveying programs for handheld HPs came out.

The bearing and quadrant code are prompted for, and all input (and output) is in Degrees,minutes and seconds (D.ms) format. After each input the [R/S] key is stroked. Our programming also includes the option to use azimuths instead of bearings . . . the azimuth is input (D.ms) and the [R/S] key is stroked. These options are presented at the beginning of each COGO program, and selected by your answer to the prompt, AZ=0 BRG=1, where you enter either 0 (work in azimuth) or 1 (work in bearings) and then stroke the [R/S] key.

storing/recalling coordinates by point number

A great advantage with the HP35s is the ability to store and recall coordinates by point numbers. We used LBL P (for point) for the program that allows you to do both the storage and recalling. The program uses the INPUT functions to prompt for the item needed. For instance, the traverse program will prompt P? at the beginning, followed by the prompts for N? and E?, after each number is input you stroke [R/S]. If you are using LBL P as a stand-alone program for storing or recalling points, **make sure Flag 10 is clear before starting. (after verifying the LN# you can modify the program to automatically clear Flag 10 by inserting the line CF 10 as new line 2).**

That's easy, but what if you want to start with an already stored point? The point number is input, but you stroke [+/-] before stroking [R/S], and the coordinates are recalled. The program steps for LBL P begin on page 9P.

PROGRAM: STORE OR RECALL POINTS

	PROMPT	INSTRUCTIONS	KEYSTROKES	OUTPUT
1		Clear Flag 10, Begin the program	[◄] [∧] [2] [.] [0] [XEQ] [P] [ENTER]	
2a	P?	To store a point input the point #	point # [R/S]	# is stored and prompts continue at step 3
OR				
2b	P?	To recall a point input the point # as a negative number **If this option is used the program will continue from here. Option 2a will bring up the additional prompts at 3 and 4**	point # [+/-] [R/S]	# is recalled and parent program will continue from here
3	N?	Input the north coordinate	north coord [R/S]	
4	E?	Input the east coordinate	east coord [R/S]	parent program will continue from here, OR
5		**If just using LBL P to input points,** stroke [R↓] to view and check coordinates	[R↓]	NORTH COORDINATE EAST COORDINATE

Let's clear Flag 10 (⬛ ⌃ 2 · 0) and try an example of storing points . . .
Point #4, N= 502.27, E= 627.45 Point #5, N= 204.63, E= 424.56:

EXAMPLE: STORE POINTS

	PROMPT	INSTRUCTIONS	KEYSTROKES	OUTPUT
1		Clear Flag 10, Begin the program	⬛ ⌃ 2 · 0 XEQ P ENTER	
2a	P? #	(The last used point # will be shown in the x-register)	4 R/S	Next prompt
3	N? #	(The last used north coordinate will be shown in the x-register) Input the new north coordinate	5 0 2 · 2 7 R/S	Next prompt
4	E? #	(The last used east coordinate will be shown in the x-register) Input the new east coordinate	6 2 7 · 4 5 R/S	parent program will continue from here
5		View and check coordinates	R↓	502.2700 627.4500
1		Begin the program	XEQ P ENTER	
2a	P? #	(The last used point # will be shown in the x-register)	5 R/S	Next prompt 4.0000
3	N? #	(The last used north coordinate will be shown in the x-register) Input the new north coordinate	2 0 4 · 6 3 R/S	Next prompt 502.2700
4	E? #	(The last used east coordinate will be shown in the x-register) Input the new east coordinate	4 2 4 · 5 6 R/S	Next prompt 627.4500
5		View and check coordinates	R↓	204.6300 424.5600

Okay, now let's try recalling those same points . . .

	PROMPT	INSTRUCTIONS	KEYSTROKES	OUTPUT
1		Clear Flag 10, Begin the program	⬛ ⌃ 2 · 0 XEQ P ENTER	
2a	P? #	(The last used point # will be shown in the x-register)	4 +/- R/S	502.2700 627.4500
1		Begin the program	XEQ P ENTER	
2a	P? #	(The last used point # will be shown in the x-register)	5 +/- R/S	204.6300 424.5600

When LBL P is being used as a subroutine by another program, traverse for instance, you will be traversing to the next point (which calculates the coordinates) and then prompted P? for the number to store it under. Instead of writing down the coordinates as you go you can just continue with the traverse, noting the point numbers on your sketch, and then recall them later to note the coordinate values.

let's talk about traverse types

A traverse may be thought of as either a "*closed*" or an "*open*" traverse. For use with this program, a **CLOSED traverse** may be either of **two** types. What we will call the **Type A** is similar to the one shown to the right.

In this type of traverse, the line from #1 to #2 is usually a known line which is included in the traverse. The two points used would be part of a property or monument line, and the basis of bearings would be the bearing (or azimuth) of the line. This type of traverse also closes back to the original point of beginning, and allows the turning of a closing angle, which is turned at the first (and last) point, foresighting the second point.

What we will consider to be a **Type B** closed traverse is one which begins at one known point and ends at another known point. For this type (previous page) the basis of bearings is usually obtained by backsighting another known point.

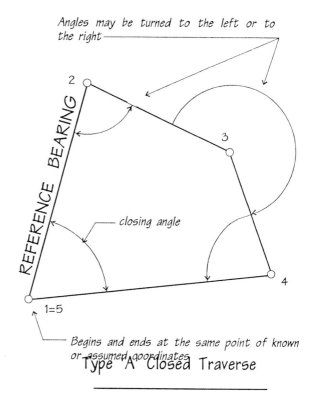

Angles may be turned to the left or to the right

closing angle

1=5

Begins and ends at the same point of known or assumed coordinates

Type "A" Closed Traverse

Type 'B' Closed Traverse

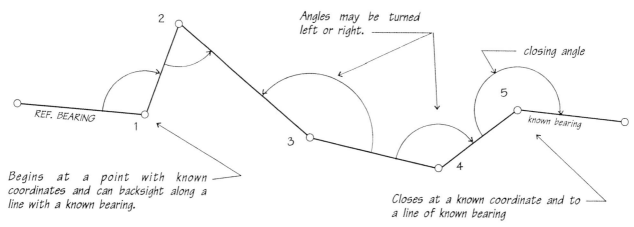

Angles may be turned left or right.

closing angle

REF. BEARING

known bearing

Begins at a point with known coordinates and can backsight along a line with a known bearing.

Closes at a known coordinate and to a line of known bearing

An *OPEN TRAVERSE* is one which, while it may begin at a known point, does **NOT** close to any point or line which allows adjustment of the traverse.

An *OPEN TRAVERSE* may also be considered as being an 'unfinished' traverse, in that it could later be used as a portion of a traverse which will be closed.

While an open traverse can **not** be closed, the Type 'B' closed traverse can. When you get to the end of the traverse, you can use the interfacing features of an **inversing during a traverse** program *(page 34)* to calculate the distance and bearing from your end point to the coordinates of the point it is trying to match. A closure routine is essentially useless in this case, since it does not enclose an area (even though one is calculated). The precision, in this case, is the total distance traversed divided by the length of the error of closure.

Often the NCEES test questions will require you to calculate a small traverse before you can answer the question, but the question will be to determine the precision of the traverse or the area the traverse encloses.

The precision of a closed traverse can be calculated by dividing the sum of the distances by the distance of the closure error. We have included a 'closure' routine, LBL K, which may be used immediately after running the traverse calculations and will complete the needed information. It calculates the error of closure, area and precision.

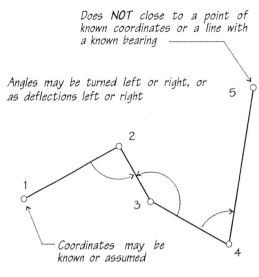

An Open Traverse

The programming instructions begin below, and we have written them to include the use of the closure routine as a part of doing the traverse. Following that, we have proceeded to the inversing program. That program has been made flexible enough to interface with the traverse, do individual inverses or to be used for inversing layout ties. We recommend that you read through this whole group before beginning to input the programs. Then take a break on the program input before tackling the intersections. Program steps for LBL T begin on page 9P.

PROGRAM: TRAVERSE

	PROMPT	INSTRUCTIONS	KEYSTROKES	OUTPUT
1		Begin the traverse program	[XEQ] [T] [ENTER]	
2	AZ=0 BRG=1	**Selection Prompt** To work in Azimuth mode, input 0. To work in Bearing/Quad mode input 1.	[0] or [1], then [R/S]	
3	P?	To begin with an already stored point, input the point number and press [+/-] [R/S] To skip this prompt, input # and press [R/S]	#[+/-][R/S] or #[0][R/S]	shows last point # used
4	N?	If starting from a new point, input the North coordinate of the beginning point.	[R/S]	shows last northing used
5	E?	If starting from a new point, input the East coordinate of the beginning point.	[R/S]	shows last easting used

(Continued on next page)

	PROMPT	INSTRUCTIONS	KEYSTROKES	OUTPUT
6a	AZIMUTH	**If Azimuth mode was selected** Input the azimuth that defines the direction of the first course.	R/S	
	OR			
6b	BEARING	**If Bearing/Quad mode was selected (a)** Input the value of the bearing that defines the direction of the first course.	R/S	
6b	QUAD CODE	**If Bearing/Quad mode was selected (b)** Input the quadrant code for the bearing that was just input.	R/S	
	THEN			
7	DISTANCE	Input the distance for this course.	R/S	NNNNN.NNNN
			R/S	EEEEE.EEEE
8	P?	Input the point number for the point	R/S	
		Returns to the prompt for the direction of the next course (step 6 above)		
		Continue through the remaining courses of the traverse, repeating steps 5 and 6, until you have finished the calculations of the coordinates back to the beginning		

Now you can run a traverse. Tests don't usually ask you what the coordinates of a given figure are, they want to know the precision, or the area, or the error of closure. The next program in this group gives you all of those and throws in the sum of the traverse's legs too.

Calculate the traverse, closing back to the beginning point, then do the closure routine.

PROGRAM: TRAVERSE CLOSURE

	PROMPT	INSTRUCTIONS	KEYSTROKES	OUTPUT
7		**Begin the closure output**	XEQ K ENTER	
8		CLOSE ERROR reminder prompt	R/S	DIRECTION DISTANCE
9		PRCSN 1: reminder prompt	R/S	PRECISION RATIO
10		AREA: reminder prompt	R/S	AREA
11		SUM H DIST: reminder prompt	R/S	PERIMETER DIST.
		When finished with the calculations	C	

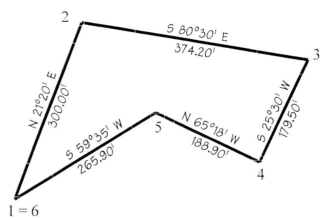

Example/Exercise 8: Calculate the coordinates for points 2 through 6 in the figure to the right, then calculate the error of closure, precision and area.

N 400
E 600

PROMPT	INSTRUCTIONS	KEYSTROKES	OUTPUT
	Begin the traverse program	XEQ T ENTER	
AZ=0 BRG=1	The example is in Bearing/Quad so it's easier to work in that mode	1 R/S	
P?	Input the beginning point number	1 R/S	Next Prompt
N?	Input the North coordinate of the beginning point.	4 0 0 R/S	Next Prompt
E?	Input the East coordinate of the beginning point.	6 0 0 R/S	Next Prompt
BEARING	Input the value of the bearing that defines the direction of the first course.	2 1 . 2 0 R/S	Next Prompt
QUAD CODE	Input the quadrant code for the bearing that was just input.	1 R/S	Next Prompt
DISTANCE	Input the distance for this course.	3 0 0 R/S	N= 679.4439
		R/S	E= 709.1380
P?	Input the point # to be used	2 R/S	Next Prompt
BEARING	**Continue with the traverse, noting the coordinates as you go. When finished, calculate the closure information**	XEQ K ENTER	

	1	N:400.0000'	E:600.0000'
Check your results against these:		N 21°20'00" E 300.0000'	
	2	N:679.4439'	E:709.1380'
Closure Distance: 0.0191'		S 80°30'00" E 374.2000'	
Closure Bearing: N 27°26'31" W	3	N:617.6831'	E:1078.2060'
Closure Azimuth: 332°23'29"		S 25°30'00" W 179.5000'	
Perimeter: 1308.5000'	4	N:455.6690'	E:1000.9293'
Area: 64666.2216 sq ft		N 65°18'00" W 188.9000'	
Precision: 68424.0051	5	N:534.6041'	E:829.3121'
		S 59°35'00" W 265.9000'	
	6	N:399.9831'	E:600.0089'

inversing

Next to traversing, the most used program is probably inversing, referred to as the "reverse solution" in some countries. There are several uses for inversing . . . as a stand-alone method of determining the direction and distance between two pairs of coordinate values, to determine which way to go toward a known point as you are traversing, and of course, to stake out points from a known control point and backsite. We'll take these one at a time, starting with just a "traverse by inverse" program (LBL L, program steps begin on page 11P). Type in the program, which works like this:

PROGRAM: INVERSING

	PROMPT	INSTRUCTIONS	KEYSTROKES	OUTPUT
1		Begin the traverse by inverse program	XEQ L ENTER	
2	AZ=0 BRG=1	**Selection Prompt** To work in Azimuth mode, input 0. To work in Bearing/Quad mode input 1.	0 or 1, then R/S	
3	P?	To begin with an already stored point, input the point number and press +/- R/S. Go to step 6. For a new point input # and press R/S go to step 4.	#+/- R/S or #0 R/S	shows last point # used
4	N?	If starting from a new point, input the North coordinate of the beginning point.	R/S	shows last northing used
5	E?	If starting from a new point, input the East coordinate of the beginning point.	R/S	shows last easting used
6	P?	To inverse to an already stored point, input the point number and press +/- R/S. Go to step 9. For a new point input # and press R/S go to step 7.	#+/- R/S or #0 R/S	shows last point # used
7	N?	If starting from a new point, input the North coordinate of the beginning point.	R/S	shows last northing used
8	E?	If starting from a new point, input the East coordinate of the beginning point.	R/S	shows last easting used
9a		**If Azimuth mode was selected**	R/S	AZIMUTH
	OR			
9b		**If Bearing/Quad mode was selected**	R/S	BEARING
10		**If Bearing/Quad mode was selected**	R/S	QUAD CODE
11			R/S	DISTANCE
12			R/S	NORTHING
13			R/S	EASTING
14			R/S	
	P?	Returns to the step 6 for input of the next point. Inverse will be from the PREVIOUS point.		

Example / Exercise 9:

In the example/exercise on page 31 we calculated the coordinates for points 1 through 6, so we can use those for an exercise by inversing around the points already stored. Work in azimuth and note the azimuths and distances. Note that your answers will not be *exactly* the same as the traverse.

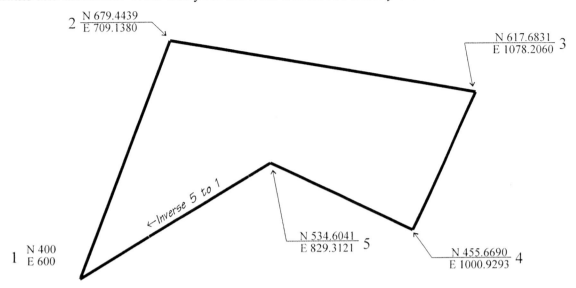

	PROMPT	INSTRUCTIONS	KEYSTROKES	OUTPUT
1		Begin the traverse by inverse program	[XEQ] [L] [ENTER]	
2	AZ=0 BRG=1	**Selection Prompt** To work in Azimuth mode, input 0. To work in Bearing/Quad mode input 1.	[1], then [R/S]	
3	P?	Beginnning with point number 1, stroke [+/-] [R/S]. Go to step 6.	[1] [+/-] [R/S]	shows last point # used
6	P?	Inverse to #2, already stored point, stroke [+/-] [R/S]. Go to step 9b.	[2] [+/-] [R/S]	shows last point # used
7	N?	If starting from a new point, input the North coordinate of the beginning point.	[R/S]	shows last northing used
8	E?	If starting from a new point, input the East coordinate of the beginning point.	[R/S]	shows last easting used
9b		**If Bearing/Quad mode was selected**	[R/S]	21.1954
10		**If Bearing/Quad mode was selected**	[R/S]	1
11			[R/S]	299.9964
12			[R/S]	N= 679.4439
			[R/S]	E= 709.1280
			[R/S]	
	P?	Returns to the step 6 for input of the next point. Inverse will be from the LAST point.		

Continue through the remainder of the traverse, checking your answers with those on page 31.

A separate program (LBL X, below) let's you inverse to another (known) point while you are traversing. The result is not saved, and does not affect the traverse in progress. For a stand-alone program for staking out points, there is LBL S, program steps on page 11P, and the instruction set on page 35. This program (LBL S) will output the direction and distance from the **current** traverse point.

another short program to input

X001	LBL X	⏎ XEQ X	
X002	CF 10	⬅ ∧ 2 · 0	
X003	CLSTK	⏎ ← 5	
X004	RCL N	RCL N	
X005	STO H	⏎ RCL H	
X006	RCL E	RCL E	
X007	STO I	⏎ RCL I	
X008	XEQ P001	XEQ P 0 0 1	
X009	N-H	EQN Then stroke RCL before each alpha input	
X010	E-I	EQN Then stroke RCL before each alpha input	
X011	XEQ T062	XEQ T 0 6 2	
X012	STO D	⏎ RCL D	
X013	x<>y	x↔y	
X014	STO A	⏎ RCL A	

X015	XEQ A004	XEQ A 0 0 4	
X016	RCL H	RCL H	
X017	STO N	⏎ RCL N	
X018	RCL I	RCL I	
X019	STO E	⏎ RCL E	
X020	RCL Z	RCL Z	
X021	x=0?	⏎ MODE 6	
X022	VIEW A	⬅ R↓ A	
X023	FS? 2	⬅ ∧ 3 2	
X024	VIEW B	⬅ R↓ B	
X025	FS? 2	⬅ ∧ 3 2	
X026	VIEW Q	⬅ R↓ Q	
X027	VIEW D	⬅ R↓ D	
X028	GTO T017	GTO T 0 1 7	
X029	RTN	⬅ XEQ	

LN=93

PROGRAM: INVERSING – USED DURING A TRAVERSE

	PROMPT	INSTRUCTIONS	KEYSTROKES	OUTPUT
1		To do an inverse during a traverse, set Flag 4 before beginning	⬅ ∧ 1 4 XEQ X ENTER	
2	P?	**Input the point number.** If this is an already stored point number, stoke ⌹ before R/S and go to step 5	# or ⌹# then R/S	
3	NORTHING	Input the North coordinate of the ending point.	R/S	
4	EASTING	Input the East coordinate of the ending point.	R/S	
5		**If Azimuth mode was selected**	R/S	AZIMUTH
	OR			
5a		**If Bearing/Quad mode was selected**	R/S	BEARING
5b		**If Bearing/Quad mode was selected**	R/S	QUAD CODE
6			R/S	DISTANCE
7			R/S	NORTHING
8			R/S	EASTING
9	BEARING	Returns you to the traverse program at the proper prompt to continue with the next traverse course	R/S	

PROGRAM: STAKEOUT

	PROMPT	INSTRUCTIONS	KEYSTROKES	OUTPUT
1		Begin the stakeout routine	XEQ S ENTER	
2	P?	Input the point number to be used for the instrument position	R/S	
3	N?	Input the North coordinate of the instrument position	R/S	
4	E?	Input the East coordinate of the instrument position	R/S	
5	P?	Input the point number to be used for the backsight position	R/S	
6	N?	Input the North coordinate of the backsight position	R/S	
7	E?	Input the East coordinate of the backsight position	R/S	AZIMUTH DISTANCE
		This is the azimuth to put into the instrument while you sight the backsite point. The distance may be used to check accuracy.		
8	P?	Input the point number to be used for the position you are staking out	R/S	
9	N?	Input the North coordinate of the position you are staking out	R/S	
10	E?	Input the East coordinate of the position you are staking out	R/S	AZIMUTH DISTANCE
11		**Stakeout the point**	R/S	
		Returns you to step 8 for the next point's input		

Exercise 10:

Use the stakeout program to calculate the stakeout ties to the lot and building corners in the figure on the opposite page if the coordinates of the control point are N 500.00 and E 1100.00. Backsight N 702.89 and E 859.33. The coordinates of the lot corners are: Southwest corner N 527.9300, E 1214.0600; Southeast corner N 504.6886, E 1307.2763 and the building corner coordinates are N 553.4100, E 1235.8721.

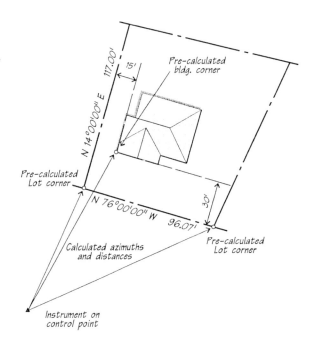

Backsight Az? _____

Distance and azimuth to the southwest Lot Corner

_____

Distance and azimuth to the southeast Lot Corner

_____

Distance and azimuth to the building corner

_____

intersection solutions

The solutions to intersections problems are needed all of the time in surveying. We use an intersection formula to find out where two lines cross, then make that point the new IP or lot corner. Or, we need to know how far a point is offset from a given line, and at what distance from the line's origin. Next to just plain traversing, this is the most used type of calculation in surveying.

We've included all of the normal solutions, the type being chosen as part of the input and then worked by use of flags instead of using up four separate lables plus one for coordinate input. This makes one longer program, but is actually shorter than the total of the other five needed the other way.

The illustration to the right allows using all four of the intersection types for trying out the programming after you have input it. We have left everything in the 'bearing' format, rather than refer to 'directions' and distances, but you may work in either azimuth or bearing for your input and output.

Input for the program begins with prompts for the beginning and ending coordinate pairs, in this case N_1, E_1 and N_2, E_2 . The point to be output as the intersection will be N_3, E_3 for the bearing-bearing, bearing-distance and the distance-distance solutions.

For all of the distance/offset solutions, the intersection point will be somewhere along the bearing line from points 1 to 3, or that same line produced past 3, shown as N6,E6, N7,E7 and N8, E8.

The step-by-step program input/output instructions begin on the next page. We've used the program keystroke instructions to solve some of the various problems as shown in the table to the right. The user should solve the remaining Bearing-Offset problems for practice.

This is a program where we suggest that you input part of it, take a break, then complete the rest at a different sitting, to help reduce program input errors.

1	150.00	175.00
2	125.00	400.00
3	To be calculated	
4	300.00	200.00
5	400.00	150.00
6	To be calculated	
7	To be calculated	
8	To be calculated	

PROGRAM: Intersections

	PROMPT	INSTRUCTIONS	KEYSTROKES	OUTPUT
1		Begin the intersection program	XEQ I ENTER	
3	P?	This is the beginning point, input the point number and press +/- R/S. Go to step 4. For a new point input # and press R/S and go to step 4.	# +/- R/S or # 0 R/S	shows last point # used
3	N?	If starting from a new point, input the North coordinate of the beginning point.	R/S	shows last northing used
3	E?	If starting from a new point, input the East coordinate of the beginning point.	R/S	shows last easting used
4	P?	This is the ending point, input the point number and press +/- R/S or R/S.	# +/- R/S or # 0 R/S	shows last point # used
5	N?	If starting from a new point, input the North coordinate of the ending point.	R/S	shows last northing used
6	E?	If starting from a new point, input the East coordinate of the ending point.	R/S	shows last easting used
7	AZ=0 BRG=1	**Selection Prompt** To work in Azimuth mode, input 0. To work in Bearing/Quad mode input 1.	1, then R/S	
8a	AZ-AZ=1 OR BRG-BRG=1 Depending on 7	**If Azimuth mode was selected** OR **If Bearing/Quad mode was selected**	To select this type, input 1, to NOT select this type, NO input. Stroke R/S	
8b	AZ-DIST=1 OR BRG-DIST=1 Depending on 7	**If Azimuth mode was selected** OR **If Bearing/Quad mode was selected**	To select this type, input 1, to NOT select this type, NO input. Stroke R/S	
8c	DIST-DIST=1	**To select this type, input 1 to NOT select this type, NO input.**	To select this type, input 1, to NOT select this type, NO input. Stroke R/S	
8d	AZ-OS=1 OR BRG-OS=1 Depending on 7	**If Azimuth mode was selected** OR **If Bearing/Quad mode was selected**	To select this type, input 1, to NOT select this type, NO input. Stroke R/S	

At this point you have input the beginning and ending coordinates, selected the type of input (azimuth or bearing) and the type of intersection you want to do. Separate instructions are given for each type of intersection solution (on the following pages), as examples, and will use either azimuth or bearing input. If you chose a different input than that shown in the example, the only difference will be the prompts for the directions. Output, in all cases will be the bearing (or azimuth) and distance from the beginning point to the intersection point, the coordinates of the intersection, then bearing (or azimuth) and distance to the ending point.

PROGRAM: Intersections (continued) BEARING – BEARING Selected

Working the problem as an input example, use the figure below.

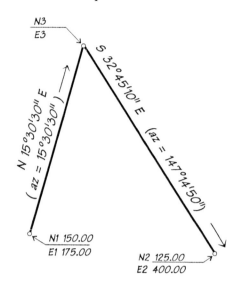

This example uses the input as bearing and quad code with the matching output.

	PROMPT	KEYSTROKES	OUTPUT
9a	BEARING	[1][5][·][3][0][3] [R/S]	
9b	QUAD CODE	[1] [R/S]	
10a	BEARING	[3][2][·][4][5][1] [R/S]	
10b	QUAD CODE	[2] [R/S]	B= 15.3030
11		[R/S]	Q= 1.0000
12		[R/S]	D = 235.4673
13		[R/S]	N= 376.8943
14		[R/S]	E= 237.9589
15		[R/S]	B= 32.4510
16		[R/S]	Q= 2.0000
17		[R/S]	D= 299.5130
18	P?	[R/S] Returns to the intersection program for new calculations. To leave the program stroke [C]	

PROGRAM: Intersections (continued) BEARING – DISTANCE Selected

Again working the problem as an input example, use Azimuth for the input on the figure below.

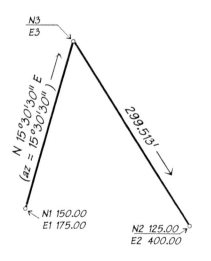

	PROMPT	KEYSTROKES	OUTPUT
9	AZIMUTH	[1][5][·][3][0][3] [R/S]	
10b	DISTANCE	[2][9][9][·][5][1][3] [R/S]	A= 15,3030
11			D= 235.4672
12		[R/S]	N= 376.8943
13		[R/S]	E= 237.9589
14		[R/S]	A= 147.1450
15		[R/S]	D= 299.5130
		[R/S] Returns to the intersection program for new calculations. To leave the program stroke [C]	

PROGRAM: Intersections (continued) DISTANCE – DISTANCE Selected

Working the problem as an input example, use the figure below and select azimuth for the directions.

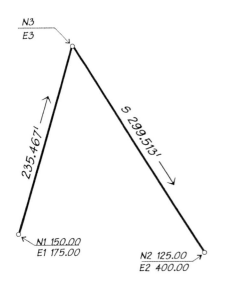

	PROMPT	KEYSTROKES	OUTPUT
9	DISTANCE	2 3 5 . 4 6 7 R/S	
10	DISTANCE	2 9 9 . 5 1 3 R/S	A= 15.3030
12		R/S	D= 235.4670
13		R/S	N= 376.8943
14		R/S	E= 237.9589
15		R/S	A= 147.1450
16		R/S	D= 299.5130
		R/S Returns to the intersection program for new calculations. To leave the program stroke C	

NOTE: The last two types may have 2 possible solutions. For the 2nd solution in Bearing-Distance, just reverse the direction of the bearing and re-run the calculation. For the 2nd solution on the Distance-Distance type, run it backwards.

PROGRAM: Intersections (continued) BEARING – OFFSET Selected

For this one, we've calculated the offset to the second point as the example (N6, E6).

We're going to use the other two in the exercise.

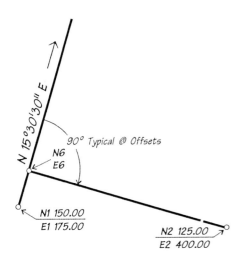

	PROMPT	KEYSTROKES	OUTPUT
9	AZIMUTH	1 5 . 3 0 3 R/S	A= 15.3030
10		R/S	D= 36.0704
11		R/S	N= 184.7571
12		R/S	E= 184.6444
13		R/S	A= 105.3030
14		R/S	D= 233.4926
		R/S Returns to the intersection program for new calculations. To leave the program stroke C	

calculating missing sides

It sometimes happens that some of the dimensions for a traverse (or deed) are missing. In order to solve for *any* missing part of a traverse, we have to first **assume** that the traverse closes, because any part we calculate is based upon the information furnished by the other parts, and will only work on a *closed* figure. When we calculate our answer, we are *forcing* a closure.

One side missing is the most obvious example of solving for a missing part. We have everything except the closing line.

If, using the traverse program, coordinates are put on each of the known corners, it is a simple matter to obtain the missing side's length and direction by inversing from #4 to #1.

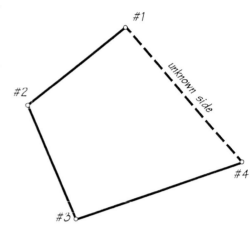

Adjacent missing Parts. It also happens that you are missing TWO parts of a traverse and need to simultaneously solve for both parts. You can do this by reducing the traverse to a point where the difference in latitudes and departures of the *known* parts may be used to solve the two missing sides.

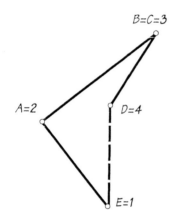

The illustration to the left shows the basic principles involved, and we can use the formulas

$$a = \frac{y\,(sinB) - x\,(cos\,B)}{sin(B - A)}$$

or

$$b = \frac{x\,(cosA) - y\,(sinA)}{sin(B - A)}$$

These formulas solve for missing lengths of two adjacent sides, and may also be re-written in the form

$$sin\,(B - A) = \frac{y\,(sinB) - x\,(cos\,B)}{a} = \frac{x\,(cosA) - y\,(sinA)}{b}$$

When we have the sides and need to solve for the missing bearings. If you look at these formulas, you will notice that they are the formulas for doing a bearing-bearing and bearing-distance intersection. Additional needed information, from that point on, may be solved through the use of the Law of Sines. The Law of Cosines is used for solving distance-distance intersections.

Non-adjacent unknowns also occur. It may be that the missing parts will fall on sides of the traverse which are **not** adjacent to each other. You can arrive at a solution by *re-arrangement* of the traverse. For purposes of *temporary* coordinate values you can connect the sides with known bearings AND distances together, making the missing sides adjacent.

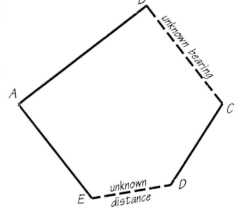

The first step is to ignore the unknown courses and connect up all of the courses with *both* known bearings and distances. Simply rearrange the figure, leaving out the unknown sides.

As you can see below, it doesn't matter which part goes where, the figure leaves one side which may be inversed.

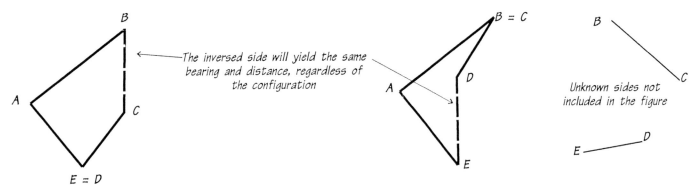

Calculate coordinates for the points in the rearranged figure and inverse for a closure (above). Next, the inversed side, combined with the two sides that contain unknowns, will form a figure like the one shown to the right. *This* figure may now be solved as a triangle, or as an intersection problem (in the case illustrated, use bearing-distance).

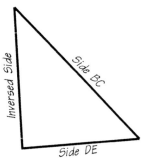

Once the unknowns are resolved, re-assemble the original figure and calculate actual coordinates for the angle points.

So, how would something like this happen in the first place? Consider the following exerpt from a deed written about 50 years ago, when all of the properties in the area were farm lands:

> . . . Thence, N 22°25' E 342.67 feet to a point in that line common to the property now or formerly owned by George W. Brown, as shown in that certain Grant Deed recorded May 16, 1923 in Book 243 of Official Records of Bohunk County at page 22; thence along said common line 435.96 feet to the most westerly line of the Smith property as shown in that certain Quitclaim Deed recorded September 24, 1940 in Book 136 of Official Records of Bohunk County at page 209; thence, along last said westerly line S 47°22' W to the point of beginning, containing . . .

And there you have a not uncommon source of unknown lines. The distance along Brown's line is known but not the direction, and Smith's line has a direction but not a distance.

When solving a problem like this it's important to understand that the answers (as in the simple inverse for closure) are a 'forced' solution. It is only as accurate as the other information that was used to calculate it. The answer is not 'real' by any definition but is a solution based on the known information. A look at Brown's deed might give a bearing for that line, but was written at a different time and not necessarily based on the same basis of bearings. Without more information being known there is no way to check the answers.

Exercise 11

Using the figure shown to the right, solve for the unknowns, then calculate and close the boundary.

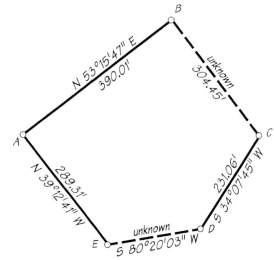

1. What is the bearing of line B-C? _____

2. What is the distance for lint D-E? _____

3. What is the area of the enclosed property? _____

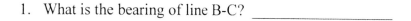

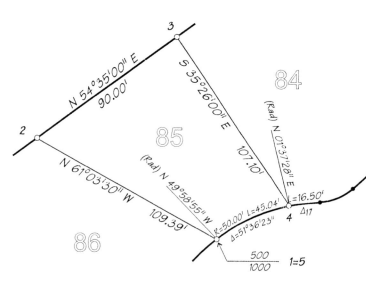

4. Calculate the coordinates for Lot 85, shown to the left.

Pt #	North Coordinate	East Coordinate
2		
3		
4		

5. What is the area of Lot 85?

_____ Sq. Ft.

6. Calculate the coordinates for point #6, the B.C and E.C. of the curve in the figure to the right. B.C. Sta = 115+24.96

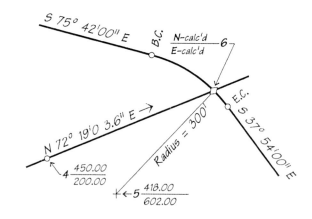

7 .
  Radius = _____

  Delta = _____

  Length = _____

  Tangent = _____

  Chord = _____

  External = _____

  Mid-Ordinate = _____

Calculate the curve data for the curve

curve to curve intersection

The intersection program will calculate the intersection point along the arcs of two curves when the two radii and the point numbers of the radius points are known. Use the Distance-Distance option, with the radii being the two distances, to solve the problem.

Input is ALWAYS counter-clockwise, as seen from the intersection point.

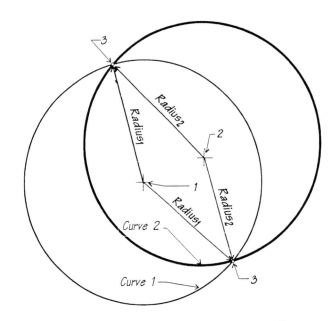

line to curve intersection

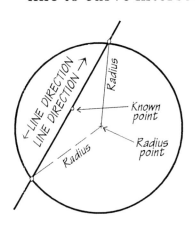

You need to know the radius of the curve, the coordinates of its radius point, a known coordinate at any location on the line, and the direction of the line.

If the line point is on the *inside* of the curve, the direction of the line is given **toward** the point of intersection that you want to calculate.. If *outside* the curve, it is often easiest to set a point on line that is inside the curve to avoid confusion.

Both of these problems can also be solved by calculation as triangle problems, although the intersection is quicker.

slope staking

Surveyors tend to think of slope staking as a trial-and-error field exercise, as it is done in the field. On a test it has to be generalized, and unless the illustration includes a grid at a given scale so you can count the squares for distance and elevation, the quick way is to use the intersection program. They will have to give you a picture with all of the slopes, distances, etc. to even formulate a problem.

Okay, turn the slopes into azimuths, calculate the distance to the far side of the v-ditch, work the slopes to get an elevation for that point.

Using the elevations as the north coordinates and the distances as the east coordinates, calculate the intersection at the catch point. It's just an azimuth-azimuth intersection problem.

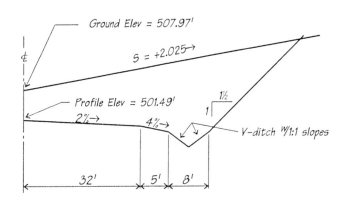

trouble-shooting your programs

If you are running a program and encounter an error message, stop and stroke ⟨◄⟩⟨R/S⟩ to go into program mode. The calculator will have stopped at the point that is causing the problem.

In the case shown, "NONEXISTENT" will indicate that you have a label missing . . . You didn't input a program that the calculator is looking for yet. "DIVIDE BY 0" would usually mean that an equation or program step is trying to divide by an empty register, and "INVALID EQN" tells you that something is wrong with an equation, maybe an extra parentheses or a missing one. Correct the error and try running the program again. If the program is correct, the LN and CK numbers (see chart on page 44) should be the same as shown in the chart.

If you need to take a break while programming, stroke ⟨C⟩ to leave program mode and then stroke ⟨◄⟩⟨C⟩ to turn the calculator off. When you come back, turn the calculator back on and stroke ⟨◄⟩⟨R/S⟩ to go into program mode. You will be at the same place you left off.

During a programming session you can go to any particular step by stroking ⟨◄⟩⟨XEQ⟩⟨·⟩. This brings up a prompt display like the one to the right. Type in the step you want to go to (i.e. 0027) and when you go into program mode you will be at that step.

answers to the exercises

Exercise 1 (page 5)
1. 147°24'23"   2. 90°53'15"   3. N 40°07'18" E (az = 40°07'18")   4. S 82°58'18" W (az = 262°58'18")

Exercise 2 (page 5,6)
1. 117°41'34"   2. 140°18'31"   3. 63°54'38"   4. 117°35'20"   5. 80°13'11"   6. S 04°20'46" E
7. S 78°09'18" E   8. 223°49'17"   9. .9550   10. –3.7652   11. .9994   12. –17.1423

Exercise 3 (page 10)
1. BVC station 13+50.00 elevation 99.750 high point station 14+70.00 elevation 100.950
EVC station 16+50 elevation 98.25

2. Calculate the elevations for the following stations:

14+20 100.74 14+50 100.92   15+22 100.72   15+50 100.42   16+10 99.32

3.   At what station will the elevation 100.58 occur?   14+03.37 & 15+36.63

Exercise 4 (page 12)
1.   BVC @ Station 12+05.56, Elevation BVC 124.11,
     high point Station 14+27.78, elevation 126.33, EVC @ Station 16+05.56, Elevation 124.91

2. 12+00 _124.00_   12+50 _124.91_   13+00 _125.60_   13+50 _126.06_   14+00 _126.30_

14+50 _126.31_   15+00 _126.10_   15+50 _125.66_   16+00 _125.00_

Exercise 5 (page 15)

	1.		2.		3.		4.
Radius =	**510.23**	Radius =	**400.00**	Radius =	**200.00'**	Radius =	16,127.45
Delta =	27°45'25"	Delta =	34°44'59"	Delta =	2°56'21"	Delta =	**1°25'16"**
Length =	247.18'	Length =	242.60'	Length =	**10.26'**	Length =	400.01'
Tangent =	126.07'	Tangent =	**125.16'**	Tangent =	5.13'	Tangent =	200.02'
Chord =	**244.77'**	Chord =	238.90'	Chord =	10.26'	Chord =	**400.00'**
External =	15.34'	External =	19.12'	External =	0.07'	External =	1.24'
Mid-Ordinate =	14.90'	Mid-Ordinate =	18.25'	Mid-Ordinate =	0.07'	Mid-Ordinate =	1.24,
		Sector =	48,519.88□'	Sector =	1,026.00□'		
		Segment =	2,920.36□'	Segment =	0.45□'		
		Fillet =	1,544.12□'	Fillet =	0.23□'		

Exercise 6 (page 18)

1.

		STATION	DEFLECTION	CHORD
Radius =	510.23'	12+19.23 B.C.	0°	0.00'
Delta =	27°45'25"	12+50	1°43'40"	30.77'
Length =	247.18	13+00	4°32'06"	80.69'
Tangent =	126.06	13+50	7°20'32"	130.41'
Chord =	244.77'	14+00	10°08'59"	179.83'
External =	15.34	14+50	12°57'25"	228.81'
Mid-Ordinate =	14.89	14+66.4 EC.	13°52'42"	244.77'

2.

		STATION	TANGENT DIST.	OFFSET
Radius =	400.00'	122+34.97	0.00'	0.00'
Delta =	34°44'59"	122+50	15.03'	0.28'
Length =	242.60'	123+00	64.74'	5.27'
Tangent =	125.16'	123+50	113.45'	16.43'
Chord =	238.90'	124+00	160.39'	33.56'
External =	19.12'	124+50	204.82'	56.42'
Mid-Ordinate =	18.25'	124+77.57 **E.C.**	228.00'	71.34'

3.

		STATION	CHORD DIST.	OFFSET
Radius =	386.31'	**53+24.37**	0.00'	0.00'
Delta =	**35°15'22"**	**53+50**	24.67'	6.95'
Length =	**237.71'**	**54+00**	73.85'	15.72'
Tangent =	**122.75'**	**54+50**	123.76'	18.08'
Chord =	233.98'	**55+00**	173.56'	13.98'
External =	19.03	**55+50**	222.41'	3.48'
Mid-Ordinate =	18.14	55+62.08 **E.C.**	233.98'	0.00'

Exercise 7 (page 24)

	1.		2.		3.		4.
Side 1	**12.163**	Side 1	**29.682**	Side 1	**15**	Side 1	**65.467**
Angle 1	**76°03'56"**	Angle 1	75°14'51"	Angle 1	**84°28'18"**	Angle 1	**84°28'18"**
Side 2	**18.364**	Side 2	**23.9162**	Side 2	21.8384	Side 2	109.4502
Angle 2	37°24'35"	Angle 2	**60°19'18"**	Angle 2	**36°12'30"**	Angle 2	32°17'00"
Side 3	19.432	Side 3	33.0374	Side 3	25.2745	Side 3	122.0028
Angle 3	66°31'29"	Angle 3	44°25'51"	Angle 3	59°19'12"	Angle 3	**63°14'42"**
Area	108.3941	Area	343.240	Area	163.0263	Area	3,566.0253

	5.		6.
Side 1	**18.249**	Side 1	**32.416**
Angle 1	**79°22'06"**	Angle 1	**87°13'51"**
Side 2	24.6097	Side 2	38.1001
Angle 2	**40°10'30"**	Angle 2	41°32'56"
Side 3	27.8020	Side 3	48.8168
Angle 3	60°27'24"	Angle 3	**51°13'13"**
Area	220.6965	Area	616.8048

Exercise 10 (page 35)
Backsight Az? <u>310°07'54"</u>

Distance and azimuth to the southwest Lot Corner

<u>117.4298   76°14'26"</u>

Distance and azimuth to the southeast Lot Corner

<u>207.3293   88°42'16"</u>

Distance and azimuth to the building corner

<u>145.9927   68°32'26"</u>

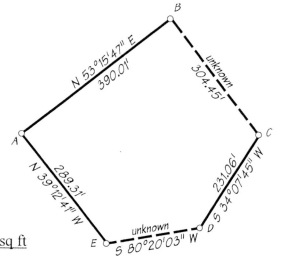

Exercise 11 (page 42)
1. What is the bearing of line B-C? <u>S 40°08'17.6" E</u>

2. What is the distance for line D-E? <u>199.0998</u>

3. What is the area of the enclosed property? <u>132,944.6772 sq ft</u>

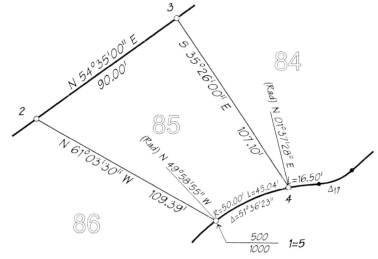

4.   Calculate the coordinates for Lot 85, shown to the left.

Pt #	North Coordinate	East Coordinate
2	552.9356	904.2714
3	605.0925	977.6177
4	517.8285	1039.7095

5.   What is the area of Lot 85?

<u>6,577.70</u>   Sq. Ft.

6.   Calculate the coordinates for point #6, the B.C and E.C. of the curve in the figure to the right..

7.

Radius =	300
Delta =	37°48'00"
Length =	197.92
Tangent =	102.71
Chord =	194.35
External =	17.10
Mid-Ordinate =	16.17

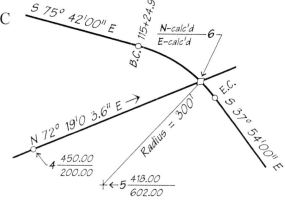

8 What is the station at the intersection of the curve and line? <u>116+68.66</u>

Vertical Curves and Grades

Step	Instruction	Keystrokes
V001	LBL V	▱ XEQ V
V002	XEQ D010	XEQ D 0 1 0
V003	SF10	◁ ∧ 1 . 0
V004	BEG STA	EQN *Then stroke* RCL *before each alpha input*
V005	STO S	▱ RCL S
V006	BEG ELEV	*EQN* *Then stroke* RCL *before each alpha input*
V007	STO E	▱ RCL E
V008	GRADE IN	EQN *Then stroke* RCL *before each alpha input*
V009	STO I	▱ RCL I
V010	CLx	▱ ← 1
V011	GRADE OUT	EQN *Then stroke* RCL *before each alpha input*
V012	STO O	▱ RCL O
V013	CLx	▱ ← 1
V014	LENGTH	EQN *Then stroke* RCL *before each alpha input*
V015	STO L	▱ RCL L
V016	x≠0?	▱ MODE 1
V017	SF 1	◁ ∧ 1 1
V018	RCL S	RCL S
V019	STO R	▱ RCL R
V020	0	0
V021	STO S	▱ RCL S
V022	FS? 1	◁ ∧ 3 1
V023	GTO V036	GTO V 0 3 6
V024	INPUT STA	EQN *Then stroke* RCL *before each alpha input*
V025	STO S	▱ RCL S
V026	RCL- R	RCL − R
V027	RCL I	RCL I
V028	100	1 0 0
V029	÷	÷
V030	x	×
V031	RCL+ E	RCL + E
V032	RCL S	RCL S
V033	x⟨⟩y	x↔y
V034	STOP	R/S
V035	GTO V024	GTO V 0 2 4
V036	RCL L	RCL L
V037	ENTER	ENTER
V038	RCL O	RCL O
V039	RCL- I	RCL − I
V040	x⟨⟩y	x↔y
V041	50	5 0
V042	÷	÷
V043	÷	÷
V044	STO M	▱ RCL M
V045	RCL I	RCL I
V046	RCLx L	RCL × L
V047	RCL I	RCL I
V048	RCL- O	RCL − O
V049	÷	÷
V050	ENTER	ENTER
V051	RCL+ R	RCL + R
V052	STO S	▱ RCL S
V053	RCL- R	RCL − R
V054	100	1 0 0
V055	÷	÷
V056	ENTER	ENTER
V057	ENTER	ENTER
V058	RCLx M	RCL × M
V059	RCL+ I	RCL + I
V060	x	×
V061	RCL+ E	RCL + E
V062	RCL S	RCL S
V063	x⟨⟩y	x↔y
V064	0	0
V065	STO S	▱ RCL S
V066	R↓	R↓
V067	STOP	R/S
V068	INPUT STA	EQN *Then stroke* RCL *before each alpha input*
V069	STO S	▱ RCL S
V070	GTO V053	GTO V 0 5 3
V071	RTN	◁ XEQ

Elevation – Find Station

Step	Instruction	Keystrokes
E001	LBL E	▱ XEQ E
E002	STO H	▱ RCL H
E003	RCL L	RCL L
E004	x=0?	▱ MODE 6
E005	GTO E047	GTO E 0 4 7
E006	RCL O	RCL O
E007	RCL- I	RCL − I
E008	100	1 0 0
E009	÷	÷
E010	RCL÷ L	RCL ÷ L
E011	STO Y	▱ RCL Y
E012	RCL E	RCL E
E013	RCL- H	RCL − H
E014	STO A	▱ RCL A

(Continued on next page)

E015	RCL Y	RCL Y
E016	2	2
E017	×	×
E018	STO K	⇄ RCL K
E019	RCL× A	RCL × A
E020	STO K	⇄ RCL K
E021	RCL I	RCL I
E022	100	1 0 0
E023	÷	÷
E024	STO X	⇄ RCL X
E025	x²	⇄ √x
E026	RCL− K	RCL − K
E027	√x	√x
E028	STO K	⇄ RCL K
E029	RCL X	RCL X
E030	+/−	+/−
E031	+	+
E032	RCL÷ Y	RCL ÷ Y
E033	RCL+ R	RCL + R
E034	STO S	⇄ RCL S
E035	RCL X	RCL X
E036	+/−	+/−
E037	RCL− K	RCL − K
E038	RCL÷ Y	RCL ÷ Y
E039	RCL+ R	RCL + R
E040	STO T	⇄ RCL T
E041	RCL S	RCL S
E042	x⟨⟩y	x↔y
E043	STOP	R/S
E044	FS? 1	⬅ ∧ 3 1
E045	GTO V036	GTO V 0 3 6
E046	RTN	⬅ XEQ
E047	RCL E	RCL E
E048	RCL− H	RCL − H
E049	RCL I	RCL I
E050	100	1 0 0
E051	÷	÷
E052	÷	÷
E053	+/−	+/−
E054	RCL+ R	RCL + R
E055	STO S	⇄ RCL S
E056	VIEW S	⬅ R↓ S
E057	0	0
E058	STO S	⇄ RCL S
E059	RTN	⬅ XEQ

─── Vertical Intersections ───

H001	LBL H	⇄ XEQ H
H002	XEQ D010	XEQ D 0 1 0
H003	SF 10	⬅ ∧ 1 · 0
H004	STA 1	EQN *Then stroke* RCL *before each alpha input*
H005	STO T	⇄ RCL T
H006	ELEV 1	EQN *Then stroke* RCL *before each alpha input*
H007	STO F	⇄ RCL F
H008	STA 2	EQN *Then stroke* RCL *before each alpha input*
H009	RCL− T	RCL − T
H010	STO M	⇄ RCL M
H011	ELEV 2	EQN *Then stroke* RCL *before each alpha input*
H012	RCL F	RCL F
H013	x⟨⟩y	x↔y
H014	−	−
H015	STO N	⇄ RCL N
H016	GRADE IN	EQN *Then stroke* RCL *before each alpha input*
H017	100	1 0 0
H018	÷	÷
H019	STO I	⇄ RCL I
H020	GRADE OUT	EQN *Then stroke* RCL *before each alpha input*
H021	100	1 0 0
H022	÷	÷
H023	STO O	⇄ RCL O
H024	RCL N	RCL N
H025	RCL O	RCL O
H026	ENTER	ENTER
H027	RCL N	RCL N
H028	x⟨⟩y	x↔y
H029	÷	÷
H030	RCL+ M	RCL + M
H031	RCL× O	RCL × O
H032	RCL I	RCL I
H033	RCL− O	RCL − O
H034	÷	÷
H035	+/−	+/−
H036	RCL+ T	RCL + T
H037	STO X	⇄ RCL X
H038	ENTER	ENTER
H039	RCL− T	RCL − T
H040	RCL× I	RCL × I
H041	RCL+ F	RCL + F

(Continued on next page)

Line	Instruction	Keystrokes
H042	RCL X	[RCL] [X]
H043	x<>y	[x↔y]
H044	RTN	[←] [XEQ]

—Circular Curves—

Line	Instruction	Keystrokes
C001	LBL C	[→] [XEQ] [C]
C002	XEQ D010	[XEQ] [D] [0] [1] [0]
C003	SF 10	[←] [∧] [1] [.] [0]
C004	DELTA	[EQN] *Then stroke* [RCL] *before each alpha input*
C005	CF 10	[←] [∧] [2] [.] [0]
C006	HMS→	[←] [8]
C007	STO D	[→] [RCL] [D]
C008	x≠0?	[→] [MODE] [1]
C009	SF 1	[←] [∧] [1] [1]
C010	INPUT R	[←] [x↔y] [R]
C011	x≠0?	[→] [MODE] [1]
C012	SF 2	[←] [∧] [1] [2]
C013	RCL D	[RCL] [D]
C014	RCL R	[RCL] [R]
C015	X	[X]
C016	x≠0?	[→] [MODE] [1]
C017	CF 1	[←] [∧] [2] [1]
C018	x≠0?	[→] [MODE] [1]
C019	CF 2	[←] [∧] [2] [2]
C020	x≠0?	[→] [MODE] [1]
C021	SF 3	[←] [∧] [1] [3]
C022	INPUT L	[←] [x↔y] [L]
C023	FS? 2	[←] [∧] [3] [2]
C024	L×180÷(π×R)	[EQN] *Then stroke* [RCL] *before each alpha input*
C025	FS? 2	[←] [∧] [3] [2]
C026	ABS	[→] [+/-]
C027	FS? 2	[←] [∧] [3] [2]
C028	STO D	[→] [RCL] [D]
C029	x≠0?	[→] [MODE] [1]
C030	CF 2	[←] [∧] [2] [2]
C031	FS? 1	[←] [∧] [3] [1]
C032	L×180÷(π×D)	[EQN] *Then stroke* [RCL] *before each alpha input*
C033	FS? 1	[←] [∧] [3] [1]
C034	ABS	[→] [+/-]
C035	FS? 1	[←] [∧] [3] [1]
C036	STO R	[→] [RCL] [R]
C037	x≠0?	[→] [MODE] [1]
C038	CF 1	[←] [∧] [2] [1]
C039	INPUT C	[←] [x↔y] [C]
C040	FS? 2	[←] [∧] [3] [2]
C041	2×ASIN(C÷ (R×2))	*input as 1 equation* [EQN] *Then stroke* [RCL] *before each alpha input*
C042	FS? 2	[←] [∧] [3] [2]
C043	ABS	[→] [+/-]
C044	FS? 2	[←] [∧] [3] [2]
C045	STO D	[→] [RCL] [D]
C046	x≠0?	[→] [MODE] [1]
C047	CF 2	[←] [∧] [2] [2]
C048	FS? 1	[←] [∧] [3] [1]
C049	C÷(2×SIN (D÷2))	*input as 1 equation* [EQN] *Then stroke* [RCL] *before each alpha input*
C050	FS? 1	[←] [∧] [3] [1]
C051	ABS	[→] [+/-]
C052	FS? 1	[←] [∧] [3] [1]
C053	STO R	[→] [RCL] [R]
C054	x≠0?	[→] [MODE] [1]
C055	CF 1	[←] [∧] [2] [1]
C056	INPUT T	[←] [x↔y] [T]
C057	FS? 2	[←] [∧] [3] [2]
C058	ATAN(T÷R)×2	[EQN] *Then stroke* [RCL] *before each alpha input*
C059	FS? 2	[←] [∧] [3] [2]
C060	ABS	[→] [+/-]
C061	FS? 2	[←] [∧] [3] [2]
C062	STO D	[→] [RCL] [D]
C063	x≠0?	[→] [MODE] [1]
C064	CF 2	[←] [∧] [2] [2]
C065	FS? 1	[←] [∧] [3] [1]
C066	T÷TAN(0.5×D)	*input as 1 equation* [EQN] *Then stroke* [RCL] *before each alpha input*
C067	FS? 1	[←] [∧] [3] [1]
C068	ABS	[→] [+/-]
C069	FS? 1	[←] [∧] [3] [1]
C070	STO R	[→] [RCL] [R]
C071	x≠0?	[→] [MODE] [1]
C072	CF 1	[←] [∧] [2] [1]
C073	CF 1	[←] [∧] [2] [1]
C074	CF 2	[←] [∧] [2] [2]
C075	RCL L	[RCL] [L]
C076	x≠0?	[→] [MODE] [1]
C077	SF 1	[←] [∧] [1] [1]
C078	RCL C	[RCL] [C]
C079	x≠0?	[→] [MODE] [1]

(Continued on next page)

C080	SF 2	[←] [∧] [1] [2]
C081	RCL T	[RCL] [T]
C082	x≠0?	[→] [MODE] [1]
C083	SF 3	[←] [∧] [1] [3]
C084	FS? 1	[←] [∧] [3] [1]
C085	R×TAN(D÷2)	EQN *Then stroke* [RCL] *before each alpha input*
C086	FS? 1	[←] [∧] [3] [1]
C087	ABS	[→] [+/_]
C088	FS? 1	[←] [∧] [3] [1]
C089	STO T	[→] [RCL] [T]
C090	FS? 1	[←] [∧] [3] [1]
C091	2×R×(SIN (D÷2))	**input as 1 equation** EQN *Then stroke* [RCL] *before each alpha input*
C092	FS? 1	[←] [∧] [3] [1]
C093	ABS	[→] [+/_]
C094	FS? 1	[←] [∧] [3] [1]
C095	STO C	[→] [RCL] [C]
C096	R×D×(π÷180)	EQN *Then stroke* [RCL] *before each alpha input*
C097	FS? 2	[←] [∧] [3] [2]
C098	ABS	[→] [+/_]
C099	FS? 2	[←] [∧] [3] [2]
C100	STO L	[→] [RCL] [L]
C101	FS? 2	[←] [∧] [3] [2]
C102	R×TAN(D÷2)	EQN *Then stroke* [RCL] *before each alpha input*
C103	FS? 2	[←] [∧] [3] [2]
C104	ABS	[→] [+/_]
C105	FS? 2	[←] [∧] [3] [2]
C106	STO T	[→] [RCL] [T]
C107	FS? 3	[←] [∧] [3] [3]
C108	R×D×(π÷180)	EQN *Then stroke* [RCL] *before each alpha input*
C109	FS? 3	[←] [∧] [3] [3]
C110	ABS	[→] [+/_]
C111	FS? 3	[←] [∧] [3] [3]
C112	STO L	[→] [RCL] [L]
C113	FS? 3	[←] [∧] [3] [3]
C114	2×R×SIN (D÷2)	**input as 1 equation** EQN *Then stroke* [RCL] *before each alpha input*
C115	FS? 3	[←] [∧] [3] [3]
C116	ABS	[→] [+/_]
C117	FS? 3	[←] [∧] [3] [3]
C118	STO C	[→] [RCL] [C]
C119	FS? 3	[←] [∧] [3] [3]
C120	RCL R	[RCL] [R]
C121	FS? 3	[←] [∧] [3] [3]
C122	TAN(D÷2)	EQN *Then stroke* [RCL] *before each alpha input*
C123	FS? 3	[←] [∧] [3] [3]
C124	x	[×]
C125	FS? 3	[←] [∧] [3] [3]
C126	ABS	[→] [+/_]
C127	FS? 3	[←] [∧] [3] [3]
C128	STO T	[→] [RCL] [T]
C129	RCL D	[RCL] [D]
C130	→HMS	[→] [8]
C131	STO I	[→] [RCL] [I]
C132	VIEW I	[←] [R↓] [I]
C133	VIEW R	[←] [R↓] [R]
C134	VIEW L	[←] [R↓] [L]
C135	VIEW C	[←] [R↓] [C]
C136	VIEW T	[←] [R↓] [T]
C137	T×TAN(D÷4)	EQN *Then stroke* [RCL] *before each alpha input*
C138	ABS	[→] [+/_]
C139	STO E	[→] [RCL] [E]
C140	VIEW E	[←] [R↓] [E]
C141	R×(1-COS (D÷2))	**input as 1 equation** EQN *Then stroke* [RCL] *before each alpha input*
C142	ABS	[→] [+/_]
C143	STO M	[→] [RCL] [M]
C144	VIEW M	[←] [R↓] [M]
C145	SF 10	[←] [∧] [1] [·] [0]
C146	AREAS	EQN *Then stroke* [RCL] *before each alpha input*
C147	PSE	[→] [x↔y]
C148	π	[←] [COS]
C149	RCL R	[RCL] [R]
C150	x²	[→] [√x]
C151	x	[×]
C152	RCL D	[RCL] [D]
C153	360	[3] [6] [0]
C154	÷	[÷]
C155	x	[×]
C156	STO S	[→] [RCL] [S]
C157	0	[0]
C158	x<>y	[x↔y]
C159	SECTOR	EQN *Then stroke* [RCL] *before each alpha input*
C160	PSE	[→] [x↔y]
C161	STOP	[R/S]
C162	RCL D	[RCL] [D]
C163	2	[2]
C164	÷	[÷]

(Continued on next page)

C165 COS	COS
C166 RCLx R	RCL × R
C167 RCLx C	RCL × C
C168 2	2
C169 ÷	÷
C170 -	−
C171 0	0
C172 x<>y	x↔y
C173 SEGMENT	EQN *Then stroke* RCL *before each alpha input*
C174 PSE	⏩ x↔y
C175 STOP	R/S
C176 RCL R	RCL R
C177 RCLx T	RCL × T
C178 RCL- S	RCL − S
C179 0	0
C180 x<>y	x↔y
C181 FILLET	EQN *Then stroke* RCL *before each alpha input*
C182 PSE	⏩ x↔y
C183 STOP	R/S
C184 MORE=0 STAKE=1	EQN *Then stroke* RCL *before each alpha input*
C185 x=0?	⏩ MODE 6
C186 GTO C190	GTO C 1 9 0
C187 x≠0?	⏩ MODE 1
C188 GTO C001	GTO C 0 0 1
C189 RTN	⏪ XEQ

End 1st Input
LN=792

C190 SF 10	⏪ ∧ 1 · 0
C191 CF 0	⏪ ∧ 2 0
C192 CF 1	⏪ ∧ 2 1
C193 CF 2	⏪ ∧ 2 2
C194 CF 3	⏪ ∧ 2 3
C195 SELECT TYPE	EQN *Then stroke* RCL *before each alpha input*
C196 PSE	⏩ x↔y
C197 CLx	⏩ ← 1
C198 DEFLECTION	EQN *Then stroke* RCL *before each alpha input*
C199 x≠0?	⏩ MODE 1
C200 SF 1	⏪ ∧ 1 1
C201 CLx	⏩ ← 1
C202 TAN-OS	EQN *Then stroke* RCL *before each alpha input*
C203 x≠0?	⏩ MODE 1
C204 SF 2	⏪ ∧ 1 2
C205 CLx	⏩ ← 1
C206 CHD-OS	EQN *Then stroke* RCL *before each alpha input*

C207 x≠0?	⏩ MODE 1
C208 SF 3	⏪ ∧ 1 3
C209 CLx	⏩ ← 1
C210 OFFSET	EQN *Then stroke* RCL *before each alpha input*
C211 STO 0	⏩ RCL O
C212 RCL+ R	RCL + R
C213 RCL÷ R	RCL ÷ R
C214 STO K	⏩ RCL K
C215 BC STA	EQN *Then stroke* RCL *before each alpha input*
C216 STO B	⏩ RCL B
C217 RCL+ L	RCL + L
C218 STO H	⏩ RCL H
C219 RCL D	RCL D
C220 2	2
C221 ÷	÷
C222 RCL÷ L	RCL ÷ L
C223 STO F	⏩ RCL F
C224 SF 10	⏪ ∧ 1 · 0
C225 INPUT STA	EQN *Then stroke* RCL *before each alpha input*
C226 RCL- B	RCL − B
C227 STO J	⏩ RCL J
C228 RCLx F	RCL × F
C229 STO A	⏩ RCL A
C230 SIN	SIN
C231 RCLx R	RCL × R
C232 2	2
C233 x	×
C234 STO C	⏩ RCL C
C235 FS? 1	⏪ ∧ 3 1
C236 DEF ANGLE	EQN *Then stroke* RCL *before each alpha input*
C237 FS? 2	⏪ ∧ 3 2
C238 TAN DIST	EQN *Then stroke* RCL *before each alpha input*
C239 FS? 3	⏪ ∧ 3 3
C240 CHD DIST	EQN *Then stroke* RCL *before each alpha input*
C241 CF 10	⏪ ∧ 2 · 0
C242 FS? 1	⏪ ∧ 3 1
C243 →HMS(A)	EQN *Then stroke* RCL *before each alpha input*
C244 FS? 2	⏪ ∧ 3 2
C245 Kx(CxCOS (A))	*input as 1 equation* EQN *Then stroke* RCL *before each alpha input*

(Continued on next page)

Step	Instruction	Keystrokes
C246	FS? 3	⬅ ⌃ 3 3
C247	KxCxCOS((D÷2)-A)	*input as 1 equation* EQN *Then stroke* RCL *before each alpha input*
C248	0	0
C249	x<>y	x↔y
C250	STOP	R/S
C251	SF 10	⬅ ⌃ 1 · 0
C252	FS? 1	⬅ ⌃ 3 1
C253	CHORD	EQN *Then stroke* RCL *before each alpha input*
C254	FS? 2	⬅ ⌃ 3 2
C255	OFFSET	EQN *Then stroke* RCL *before each alpha input*
C256	FS? 3	⬅ ⌃ 3 3
C257	OFFSET	EQN *Then stroke* RCL *before each alpha input*
C258	CF 10	⬅ ⌃ 2 · 0
C259	FS? 1	⬅ ⌃ 3 1
C260	Kx(2xRxSIN (A))	*input as 1 equation* EQN *Then stroke* RCL *before each alpha input*
C261	FS?2	⬅ ⌃ 3 2
C262	Kx(CxSIN (A))	*input as 1 equation* EQN *Then stroke* RCL *before each alpha input*
C263	FS? 3	⬅ ⌃ 3 3
C264	KxCxSIN ((D÷2)-A)	*input as 1 equation* EQN *Then stroke* RCL *before each alpha input*
C265	0	0
C266	x<>y	x↔y
C267	STOP	R/S
C268	GTO C224	GTO C 2 2 4
C269	RTN	⬅ XEQ

— **Triangle Solutions** —

Step	Instruction	Keystrokes
G001	LBL G	➡ XEQ G
G002	XEQ D010	XEQ D 0 1 0
G003	CF 4	⬅ ⌃ 2 4
G004	SF 10	⬅ ⌃ 1 · 0
G005	TYPE SELECTION	EQN *Then stroke* RCL *before each alpha input*
G006	PSE	➡ x↔y
G007	CLx	➡ ⬅ 1
G008	S1-S2-S3	EQN *Then stroke* RCL *before each alpha input*
G009	x≠0?	➡ MODE 1
G010	SF 1	⬅ ⌃ 1 1
G011	CLx	➡ ⬅ 1

Step	Instruction	Keystrokes
G012	A3-S1-A1	EQN *Then stroke* RCL *before each alpha input*
G013	x≠0?	➡ MODE 1
G014	SF 2	⬅ ⌃ 1 2
G015	CLx	➡ ⬅ 1
G016	S1-A1-A2	EQN *Then stroke* RCL *before each alpha input*
G017	x≠0?	➡ MODE 1
G018	SF 3	⬅ ⌃ 1 3
G019	CLx	➡ ⬅ 1
G020	S1-A1-S2	EQN *Then stroke* RCL *before each alpha input*
G021	x≠0?	➡ MODE 1
G022	SF 4	⬅ ⌃ 1 4
G023	CLx	➡ ⬅ 1
G024	S1-S2-A2	EQN *Then stroke* RCL *before each alpha input*
G025	x≠0?	➡ MODE 1
G026	SF 0	⬅ ⌃ 1 0
G027	SF 10	⬅ ⌃ 1 · 0
G028	FS? 1	⬅ ⌃ 3 1
G029	XEQ G227	XEQ G 2 2 7
G030	FS? 3	⬅ ⌃ 3 3
G031	XEQ G227	XEQ G 2 2 7
G032	FS? 4	⬅ ⌃ 3 4
G033	XEQ G227	XEQ G 2 2 7
G034	FS? 0	⬅ ⌃ 3 0
G035	XEQ G227	XEQ G 2 2 7
G036	FS? 1	⬅ ⌃ 3 1
G037	STO D	➡ RCL D
G038	FS? 3	⬅ ⌃ 3 3
G039	STO D	➡ RCL D
G040	FS? 4	⬅ ⌃ 3 4
G041	STO D	➡ RCL D
G042	FS? 0	⬅ ⌃ 3 0
G043	STO D	➡ RCL D
G044	FS? 2	⬅ ⌃ 3 2
G045	XEQ G233	XEQ G 2 3 3
G046	FS? 2	⬅ ⌃ 3 2
G047	STO I	➡ RCL I
G048	FS? 1	⬅ ⌃ 3 1
G049	XEQ G231	XEQ G 2 3 1
G050	FS? 1	⬅ ⌃ 3 1
G051	STO F	➡ RCL F
G052	FS? 2	⬅ ⌃ 3 2
G053	XEQ G227	XEQ G 2 2 7
G054	FS? 2	⬅ ⌃ 3 2

(Continued on next page)

G055	STO D	[→] RCL D
G056	FS? 3	[←] [^] 3 3
G057	XEQ G229	XEQ G 2 2 9
G058	FS? 3	[←] [^] 3 3
G059	STO E	[→] RCL E
G060	FS? 4	[←] [^] 3 4
G061	XEQ G229	XEQ G 2 2 9
G062	FS? 4	[←] [^] 3 4
G063	STO E	[→] RCL E
G064	FS? 0	[←] [^] 3 0
G065	XEQ G231	XEQ G 2 3 1
G066	FS? 0	[←] [^] 3 0
G067	STO F	[→] RCL F
G068	FS? 1	[←] [^] 3 1
G069	INPUT SIDE 3	EQN *Then stroke* RCL *before each alpha input*
G070	FS? 1	[←] [^] 3 1
G071	STO H	[→] RCL H
G072	FS? 2	[←] [^] 3 2
G073	XEQ G229	XEQ G 2 2 9
G074	FS? 2	[←] [^] 3 2
G075	STO E	[→] RCL E
G076	FS? 3	[←] [^] 3 3
G077	INPUT ANGLE 2	EQN *Then stroke* RCL *before each alpha input*
G078	FS? 3	[←] [^] 3 3
G079	STO G	[→] RCL G
G080	FS? 4	[←] [^] 3 4
G081	XEQ G231	XEQ G 2 3 1
G082	FS? 4	[←] [^] 3 4
G083	STO F	[→] RCL F
G084	FS? 0	[←] [^] 3 0
G085	INPUT ANGLE 2	EQN *Then stroke* RCL *before each alpha input*
G086	FS? 0	[←] [^] 3 0
G087	STO G	[→] RCL G
G088	CF 10	[←] [^] 2 . 0
G089	FS? 3	[←] [^] 3 3
G090	180-(HMS→(E)+ HMS→(G))	*input as 1 equation* EQN *Then stroke* RCL *before each alpha input*
G091	FS? 3	[←] [^] 3 3
G092	→HMS	[→] 8
G093	FS? 3	[←] [^] 3 3
G094	STO I	[→] RCL I
G095	FS? 3	[←] [^] 3 3
G096	SF 2	[←] [^] 1 2
G097	FS? 3	[←] [^] 3 3
G098	CF 3	[←] [^] 2 3
G099	FS? 0	[←] [^] 3 0
G100	ASIN((F÷D)×(SIN (HMS÷(G))))	*input as 1 equation* EQN *Then stroke* RCL *before each alpha input*
G101	FS? 0	[←] [^] 3 0
G102	→HMS	[→] 8
G103	FS? 0	[←] [^] 3 0
G104	STO I	[→] RCL I
G105	FS? 0	[←] [^] 3 0
G106	180-(HMS→(I) +HMS→(G))	*input as 1 equation* EQN *Then stroke* RCL *before each alpha input*
G107	FS? 0	[←] [^] 3 0
G108	→HMS	[→] 8
G109	FS? 0	[←] [^] 3 0
G110	STO E	[→] RCL E
G111	FS? 0	[←] [^] 3 0
G112	SF 2	[←] [^] 1 2
G113	FS? 2	[←] [^] 3 2
G114	180-(HMS→(I) +HMS→(E))	*input as 1 equation* EQN *Then stroke* RCL *before each alpha input*
G115	FS? 2	[←] [^] 3 2
G116	→HMS	[→] 8
G117	FS? 2	[←] [^] 3 2
G118	STO G	[→] RCL G
G119	FS? 2	[←] [^] 3 2
G120	D×(SIN(HMS÷(I))÷ (SIN(HMS÷(G))))	*input as 1 equation* EQN *Then stroke* RCL *before each alpha input*
G121	FS? 2	[←] [^] 3 2
G122	STO F	[→] RCL F
G123	FS? 2	[←] [^] 3 2
G124	D×(COS(HMS÷ (I)))	*input as 1 equation* EQN *Then stroke* RCL *before each alpha input*
G125	FS? 2	[←] [^] 3 2
G126	F×(COS(HMS÷ (G)))	*input as 1 equation* EQN *Then stroke* RCL *before each alpha input*
G127	FS? 2	[←] [^] 3 2
G128	+	[+]
G129	FS? 2	[←] [^] 3 2
G130	STO H	[→] RCL H
G131	FS? 4	[←] [^] 3 4

(Continued on next page)

Step	Instruction	Keystrokes
G132	2×(D×F)×(COS (HMS→(E)))	input as 1 equation [EQN] Then stroke [RCL] before each alpha input
G133	FS? 4	[⇦][⌃][3][4]
G134	STO T	[⇨][RCL][T]
G135	FS? 4	[⇦][⌃][3][4]
G136	SQRT(SQ(D)+SQ (F)-T)	input as 1 equation [EQN] Then stroke [RCL] before each alpha input
G137	FS? 4	[⇦][⌃][3][4]
G138	STO H	[⇨][RCL][H]
G139	SF 1	[⇦][⌃][1][1]
G140	SF 4	[⇦][⌃][1][4]
G141	FS? 1	[⇦][⌃][3][1]
G142	(D+F+H)÷2	[EQN] Then stroke [RCL] before each alpha input
G143	FS? 1	[⇦][⌃][3][1]
G144	STO W	[⇨][RCL][W]
G145	FS? 1	[⇦][⌃][3][1]
G146	SQRT(((W×(W-F))÷(D×H)))	input as 1 equation [EQN] Then stroke [RCL] before each alpha input
G147	FS? 1	[⇦][⌃][3][1]
G148	STO T	[⇨][RCL][T]
G149	FS? 1	[⇦][⌃][3][1]
G150	2×ACOS(T)	[EQN] Then stroke [RCL] before each alpha input
G151	FS? 1	[⇦][⌃][3][1]
G152	→HMS	[⇨][8]
G153	FS? 1	[⇦][⌃][3][1]
G154	STO I	[⇨][RCL][I]
G155	FS? 1	[⇦][⌃][3][1]
G156	ACOS(SQRT(((W×(W-D))÷(F×H))))	input as 1 equation [EQN] Then stroke [RCL] before each alpha input
G157	FS? 1	[⇦][⌃][3][1]
G158	2	[2]
G159	FS? 1	[⇦][⌃][3][1]
G160	×	[×]
G161	FS? 1	[⇦][⌃][3][1]
G162	→HMS	[⇨][8]
G163	FS? 1	[⇦][⌃][3][1]
G164	STO G	[⇨][RCL][G]
G165	FS? 1	[⇦][⌃][3][1]
G166	180-(HMS→(I) +HMS→(G))	input as 1 equation [EQN] Then stroke [RCL] before each alpha input
G167	FS? 1	[⇦][⌃][3][1]
G168	→HMS	[⇨][8]
G169	FS? 1	[⇦][⌃][3][1]
G170	STO E	[⇨][RCL][E]
G171	CF 1	[⇦][⌃][2][1]
G172	SF 10	[⇦][⌃][1][.][0]
G173	SIDE 1	[EQN] Then stroke [RCL] before each alpha input
G174	RCL D	[RCL][D]
G175	STOP	[R/S]
G176	ANGLE 1	[EQN] Then stroke [RCL] before each alpha input
G177	RCL E	[RCL][E]
G178	STOP	[R/S]
G179	SIDE 2	[EQN] Then stroke [RCL] before each alpha input
G180	RCL F	[RCL][F]
G181	STOP	[R/S]
G182	ANGLE 2	[EQN] Then stroke [RCL] before each alpha input
G183	RCL G	[RCL][G]
G184	STOP	[R/S]
G185	SIDE 3	[EQN] Then stroke [RCL] before each alpha input
G186	RCL H	[RCL][H]
G187	STOP	[R/S]
G188	ANGLE 3	[EQN] Then stroke [RCL] before each alpha input
G189	RCL I	[RCL][I]
G190	STOP	[R/S]
G191	CF 10	[⇦][⌃][2][.][0]
G192	0.5×(D×H×SIN (HMS→(I)))	input as 1 equation [EQN] Then stroke [RCL] before each alpha input
G193	STO A	[⇨][RCL][A]
G194	SF 10	[⇦][⌃][1][.][0]
G195	AREA	[EQN] Then stroke [RCL] before each alpha input
G196	RCL A	[RCL][A]
G197	STOP	[R/S]
G198	FS? 0	[⇦][⌃][3][0]
G199	XEQ G202	[XEQ][G][2][0][2]
G200	GTO G001	[GTO][G][0][0][1]
G201	RTN	[⇦][XEQ]
G202	2ND SOLUTION	[EQN] Then stroke [RCL] before each alpha input
G203	CF 10	[⇦][⌃][2][.][0]
G204	180-(HMS→(I))	[EQN] Then stroke [RCL] before each alpha input

(Continued on next page

Code	Instruction	Keystrokes
G205	RCL G	RCL G
G206	STO E	[⇄] RCL E
G207	R↓	R↓
G208	→HMS	[⇄] 8
G209	STO G	[⇄] RCL G
G210	RCL F	RCL F
G211	STO D	[⇄] RCL D
G212	180-(HMS→(E) +HMS→(G))	*input as 1 equation* EQN *Then stroke* RCL *before each alpha input*
G213	→HMS	[⇄] 8
G214	STO I	[⇄] RCL I
G215	SIN(HMS→(I))	EQN *Then stroke* RCL *before each alpha input*
G216	SIN(HMS→(G))	EQN *Then stroke* RCL *before each alpha input*
G217	÷	÷
G218	RCL× D	RCL × D
G219	STO F	[⇄] RCL F
G220	D×(COS(HMS→(I)))	*input as 1 equation* EQN *Then stroke* RCL *before each alpha input*
G221	F×(COS(HMS→(G)))	*input as 1 equation* EQN *Then stroke* RCL *before each alpha input*
G222	+	+
G223	STO H	[⇄] RCL H
G224	CF 0	[◁] [△] 2 0
G225	GTO G172	GTO G 1 7 2
G226	RTN	[◁] XEQ
G227	INPUT SIDE 1	EQN *Then stroke* RCL *before each alpha input*
G228	RTN	[◁] XEQ
G229	INPUT ANGLE 1	EQN *Then stroke* RCL *before each alpha input*
G230	RTN	[◁] XEQ
G231	INPUT SIDE 2	EQN *Then stroke* RCL *before each alpha input*
G232	RTN	[◁] XEQ
G233	INPUT ANGLE 3	EQN *Then stroke* RCL *before each alpha input*
G234	RTN	[◁] XEQ

──Point Storage and Recall ──

Code	Instruction	Keystrokes
P001	LBL P	[⇄] XEQ P
P002	INPUT P	[◁] x↔y P
P003	RCL P	RCL P
P004	x<0?	[⇄] MODE 3
P005	GTO P013	GTO P 0 1 3
P006	RCL P	RCL P
P007	STO J	[⇄] RCL J
P008	INPUT N	[◁] x↔y N
P009	INPUT E	[◁] x↔y E
P010	[N,E]	EQN *Then stroke* RCL *before each alpha input*
P011	STO(J)	[⇄] RCL .
P012	RTN	[◁] XEQ
P013	RCL P	RCL P
P014	ABS	[⇄] +/_
P015	STO J	[⇄] RCL J
P016	RCL(J)	RCL .
P017	[1,0]	EQN *Then stroke* RCL *before each alpha input*
P018	x<>y	x↔y
P019	×	×
P020	STO N	[⇄] RCL N
P021	LASTx	[⇄] ENTER
P022	[0,1]	EQN *Then stroke* RCL *before each alpha input*
P023	×	×
P024	STO E	[⇄] RCL E
P025	RTN	[◁] XEQ
P026	INPUT P	[◁] x↔y P
P027	STO J	[⇄] RCL J
P028	[N,E]	EQN *Then stroke* RCL *before each alpha input*
P029	STO(J)	[⇄] RCL .
P030	RCL N	RCL N
P031	RCL E	RCL E
P032	RTN	[◁] XEQ

──Traverse──

Code	Instruction	Keystrokes
T001	LBL T	[⇄] XEQ T
T002	XEQ D010	XEQ D 0 1 0
T003	SF 10	[◁] [△] 1 . 0
T004	AZ=0 BRG=1	EQN *Then stroke* RCL *before each alpha input*
T005	STO Z	[⇄] RCL Z
T006	x≠0?	[⇄] MODE 1
T007	SF 2	[◁] [△] 1 2
T008	CF 10	[◁] [△] 2 . 0
T009	XEQ P001	XEQ P 0 0 1
T010	RCL E	RCL E
T011	STO W	[⇄] RCL W
T012	STO O	[⇄] RCL O

Continued on next page)

Step	Instruction	Keystrokes
T013	RCL N	RCL N
T014	STO Y	⤶ RCL Y
T015	STO U	⤶ RCL U
T016	x<>y	x↔y
T017	SF 10	⇦ ^ 1 . 0
T018	RCL Z	RCL Z
T019	x=0?	⤶ MODE 6
T020	AZIMUTH	EQN *Then stroke* RCL *before each alpha input*
T021	FS? 2	⇦ ^ 3 2
T022	XEQ B001	XEQ B 0 0 1
T023	STO A	⤶ RCL A
T024	HMS→	⇦ 8
T025	DISTANCE	EQN *Then stroke* RCL *before each alpha input*
T026	STO D	⤶ RCL D
T027	STO+ S	⤶ RCL + S
T028	CF 10	⇦ ^ 2 . 0
T029	XEQ T051	XEQ T 0 5 1
T030	x<>y	x↔y
T031	STO L	⤶ RCL L
T032	STO+ N	⤶ RCL + N
T033	x<>y	x↔y
T034	STO O	⤶ RCL O
T035	STO+ E	⤶ RCL + E
T036	RCL L	RCL L
T037	RCL O	RCL O
T038	2	2
T039	÷	÷
T040	RCL+ M	RCL + M
T041	X	×
T042	+	+
T043	STO+ G	⤶ RCL + G
T044	RCL O	RCL O
T045	STO+ M	⤶ RCL + M
T046	VIEW N	⇦ R↓ N
T047	VIEW E	⇦ R↓ E
T048	XEQ P026	XEQ P 0 2 6
T049	GTO T017	GTO T 0 1 7
T050	RTN	⇦ XEQ
T051	x<>y	x↔y
T052	SIN	SIN
T053	x<>y	x↔y
T054	LASTx	⤶ ENTER
T055	COS	COS
T056	x<>y	x↔y
T057	X	×

Step	Instruction	Keystrokes
T058	x<>y	x↔y
T059	LASTx	⤶ ENTER
T060	x	×
T061	RTN	⇦ XEQ
T062	i	i ENTER
T063	x	×
T064	+	+
T065	ABS	⤶ +/−
T066	LASTx	⤶ ENTER
T067	ARG	⇦ i
T068	360	3 6 0
T069	RMDR	⇦ TAN 3
T070	→HMS	⤶ 8
T071	x<>y	x↔y
T072	RTN	⇦ XEQ

——Traverse Closure——

Step	Instruction	Keystrokes
K001	LBL K	⤶ XEQ K
K002	RCL N	RCL N
K003	RCL- Y	RCL − Y
K004	RCL E	RCL E
K005	RCL- W	RCL − W
K006	XEQ T062	XEQ T 0 6 2
K007	STO D	⤶ RCL D
K008	x<>y	x↔y
K009	180	1 8 0
K010	+	+
K011	360	3 6 0
K012	RMDR	⇦ TAN 3
K013	STO A	⤶ RCL A
K014	FS? 2	⇦ ^ 3 2
K015	XEQ A004	XEQ A 0 0 4
K016	CLOSE ERROR	EQN *Then stroke* RCL *before each alpha input*
K017	PSE	⤶ x↔y
K018	FS? 2	⇦ ^ 3 2
K019	VIEW B	⇦ R↓ B
K020	FS? 2	⇦ ^ 3 2
K021	VIEW Q	⇦ R↓ Q
K022	RCL Z	RCL Z
K023	x=0?	⤶ MODE 6
K024	VIEW A	⇦ R↓ A
K025	VIEW D	⇦ R↓ D
K026	RCL S	RCL S
K027	RCL÷ D	RCL ÷ D
K028	STO R	⤶ RCL R

(Continued on next page)

K029	PRCSN RATIO	EQN *Then stroke* RCL *before each alpha input*
K030	PSE	⤵ [x↔y]
K031	VIEW R	⬑ [R↓] [R]
K032	RCL G	[RCL] [G]
K033	ABS	⤵ [+/-]
K034	STO A	⤵ [RCL] [A]
K035	AREA	EQN *Then stroke* RCL *before each alpha input*
K036	PSE	⤵ [x↔y]
K037	VIEW A	⬑ [R↓] [A]
K038	SUM H DIST	EQN *Then stroke* RCL *before each alpha input*
K039	PSE	⤵ [x↔y]
K040	VIEW S	⬑ [R↓] [S]
K041	CF 2	⬑ [∧] [2] [2]
K042	CLSTK	⤵ [←] [5]
K043	RTN	⬑ [XEQ]

—Stakeout—

S001	LBL S	⤵ [XEQ] [S]
S002	XEQ D011	[XEQ] [D] [0] [1] [1]
S003	CF 10	⬑ [∧] [2] [.] [0]
S004	XEQ P001	[XEQ] [P] [0] [0] [1]
S005	RCL N	[RCL] [N]
S006	STO H	⤵ [RCL] [H]
S007	RCL E	[RCL] [E]
S008	STO I	⤵ [RCL] [I]
S009	XEQ P001	[XEQ] [P] [0] [0] [1]
S010	RCL N	[RCL] [N]
S011	STO V	⤵ [RCL] [V]
S012	RCL E	[RCL] [E]
S013	STO K	⤵ [RCL] [K]
S014	RCL V	[RCL] [V]
S015	RCL- H	[RCL] [−] [H]
S016	RCL K	[RCL] [K]
S017	RCL- I	[RCL] [−] [I]
S018	XEQ T062	[XEQ] [T] [0] [6] [2]
S019	STO D	⤵ [RCL] [D]
S020	x<>y	[x↔y]
S021	STO A	⤵ [RCL] [A]
S022	x<>y	[x↔y]
S023	FS? 1	⬑ [∧] [3] [1]
S024	GTO L012	[GTO] [L] [0] [1] [2]
S025	STOP	[R/S]
S026	XEQ S009	[XEQ] [S] [0] [0] [9]
S027	STOP	[R/S]
S028	RTN	⬑ [XEQ]

—Inverse—

L001	LBL L	⤵ [XEQ] [L]
L002	XEQ D011	[XEQ] [D] [0] [1] [1]
L003	SF 1	⬑ [∧] [1] [1]
L004	SF 3	⬑ [∧] [1] [3]
L005	SF 10	⬑ [∧] [1] [.] [0]
L006	XEQ L027	[XEQ] [L] [0] [2] [7]
L007	CF 10	⬑ [∧] [2] [.] [0]
L008	FS? 3	⬑ [∧] [3] [3]
L009	XEQ S004	[XEQ] [S] [0] [0] [4]
L010	CF 3	⬑ [∧] [2] [3]
L011	XEQ S005	[XEQ] [S] [0] [0] [5]
L012	RCL A	[RCL] [A]
L013	XEQ A004	[XEQ] [A] [0] [0] [4]
L014	FS? 2	⬑ [∧] [3] [2]
L015	VIEW B	⬑ [R↓] [B]
L016	FS? 2	⬑ [∧] [3] [2]
L017	VIEW Q	⬑ [R↓] [Q]
L018	RCL Z	[RCL] [Z]
L019	x=0?	⤵ [MODE] [6]
L020	VIEW A	⬑ [R↓] [A]
L021	VIEW D	⬑ [R↓] [D]
L022	VIEW N	⬑ [R↓] [N]
L023	VIEW E	⬑ [R↓] [E]
L024	FS? 4	⬑ [∧] [3] [4]
L025	GTO L034	[GTO] [L] [0] [3] [4]
L026	GTO L010	[GTO] [L] [0] [1] [0]
L027	FS? 2	⬑ [∧] [3] [2]
L028	RTN	⬑ [XEQ]
L029	AZ=0 BRG=1	EQN *Then stroke* RCL *before each alpha input*
L030	STO Z	⤵ [RCL] [Z]
L031	x≠0?	⤵ [MODE] [1]
L032	SF 2	⬑ [∧] [1] [2]
L033	RTN	⬑ [XEQ]
L034	CF 4	⬑ [∧] [2] [4]
L035	GTO L011	[GTO] [L] [0] [1] [1]
L036	RTN	⬑ [XEQ]

—Intersections—

I001	LBL I	⤵ [XEQ] [I]
I002	XEQ D010	[XEQ] [D] [0] [1] [0]
I003	CF 4	⬑ [∧] [2] [4]
I004	CF 0	⬑ [∧] [2] [0]
I005	CF 10	⬑ [∧] [2] [.] [0]
I006	XEQ P001	[XEQ] [P] [0] [0] [1]
I007	RCL N	[RCL] [N]

(Continued on next page)

Step	Instruction	Keystrokes
I008	STO Y	[↰] [RCL] [Y]
I009	RCL E	[RCL] [E]
I010	STO W	[↰] [RCL] [W]
I011	XEQ P001	[XEQ] [P] [0] [0] [1]
I012	RCL N	[RCL] [N]
I013	STO U	[↰] [RCL] [U]
I014	RCL E	[RCL] [E]
I015	STO O	[↰] [RCL] [O]
I016	RCL− W	[RCL] [−] [W]
I017	RCL U	[RCL] [U]
I018	RCL− Y	[RCL] [−] [Y]
I019	x⟨⟩y	[x↔y]
I020	XEQ T062	[XEQ] [T] [0] [6] [2]
I021	STO S	[↰] [RCL] [S]
I022	x⟨⟩y	[x↔y]
I023	HMS→	[↩] [8]
I024	STO T	[↰] [RCL] [T]
I025	CLx	[↰] [←] [1]
I026	SF 10	[↩] [∧] [1] [·] [0]
I027	AZ=0 BRG=1	[EQN] *Then stroke* [RCL] *before each alpha input*
I028	x≠0?	[↩] [MODE] [1]
I029	SF 2	[↩] [∧] [1] [2]
I030	x=0?	[↰] [MODE] [6]
I031	SF 6	[↩] [∧] [1] [6]
I032	STO Z	[↰] [RCL] [Z]
I033	CLx	[↰] [←] [1]
I034	FS? 6	[↩] [∧] [3] [6]
I035	AZ−AZ=1	[EQN] *Then stroke* [RCL] *before each alpha input* [↩] [∧] [3] [2]
I036	FS? 2	[↩] [∧] [3] [2]
I037	BRG−BRG=1	[EQN] *Then stroke* [RCL] *before each alpha input*
I038	x≠0?	[↰] [MODE] [1]
I039	SF 1	[↩] [∧] [1] [1]
I040	CLx	[↰] [←] [1]
I041	FS? 6	[↩] [∧] [3] [6]
I042	AZ−DIST=1	[EQN] *Then stroke* [RCL] *before each alpha input* [↩] [∧] [3] [2]
I043	FS? 2	[↩] [∧] [3] [2]
I044	BRG−DIST=1	[EQN] *Then stroke* [RCL] *before each alpha input*
I045	x≠0?	[↰] [MODE] [1]
I046	SF 3	[↩] [∧] [1] [3]
I047	CLx	[↰] [←] [1]
I048	DIST−DIST=1	[EQN] *Then stroke* [RCL] *before each alpha input*
I049	x≠0?	[↰] [MODE] [1]
I050	SF 4	[↩] [∧] [1] [4]
I051	CLx	[↰] [←] [1]
I052	FS? 6	[↩] [∧] [3] [6]
I053	AZ−OS=1	[EQN] *Then stroke* [RCL] *before each alpha input* [↩] [∧] [3] [2]
I054	FS? 2	[↩] [∧] [3] [2]
I055	BRG−OS=1	[EQN] *Then stroke* [RCL] *before each alpha input*
I056	x≠0?	[↰] [MODE] [1]
I057	SF 0	[↩] [∧] [1] [0]
I058	CLx	[↰] [←] [1]
I059	FS? 0	[↩] [∧] [3] [0]
I060	XEQ I139	[XEQ] [I] [1] [3] [9]
I061	FS? 1	[↩] [∧] [3] [1]
I062	XEQ I139	[XEQ] [I] [1] [3] [9]
I063	FS? 3	[↩] [∧] [3] [3]
I064	XEQ I139	[XEQ] [I] [1] [3] [9]
I065	STO C	[↰] [RCL] [C]
I066	→HMS	[↰] [8]
I067	STO A	[↰] [RCL] [A]
I068	RCL T	[RCL] [T]
I069	RCL− C	[RCL] [−] [C]
I070	STO V	[↰] [RCL] [V]
I071	90	[9] [0]
I072	STO H	[↰] [RCL] [H]
I073	+	[+]
I074	180	[1] [8] [0]
I075	−	[−]
I076	+/−	[+/−]
I077	STO K	[↰] [RCL] [K]
I078	FS? 4	[↩] [∧] [3] [4]
I079	DISTANCE	[EQN] *Then stroke* [RCL] *before each alpha input*
I080	FS? 4	[↩] [∧] [3] [4]
I081	STO D	[↰] [RCL] [D]
I082	CF 10	[↩] [∧] [2] [·] [0]
I083	FS? 0	[↩] [∧] [3] [0]
I084	S×SIN(V)	[EQN] *Then stroke* [RCL] *before each alpha input*
I085	FS? 0	[↩] [∧] [3] [0]
I086	STO G	[↰] [RCL] [G]
I087	SF 10	[↩] [∧] [1] [·] [0]
I088	FS? 1	[↩] [∧] [3] [1]
I089	XEQ I139	[XEQ] [I] [1] [3] [9]
I090	FS? 1	[↩] [∧] [3] [1]

(Continued on next page)

Step	Instruction	Keystrokes
I091	STO P	▣ RCL P
I092	FS? 3	▣ ∧ 3 3
I093	DISTANCE	EQN *Then stroke* RCL *before each alpha input*
I094	FS? 3	▣ ∧ 3 3
I095	STO G	▣ RCL G
I096	FS? 4	▣ ∧ 3 4
I097	DISTANCE	EQN *Then stroke* RCL *before each alpha input*
I098	FS? 4	▣ ∧ 3 4
I099	STO G	▣ RCL G
I100	CF 10	▣ ∧ 2 . 0
I101	FS? 0	▣ ∧ 3 0
I102	XEQ I184	XEQ I 1 8 4
I103	FS? 1	▣ ∧ 3 1
I104	XEQ I177	XEQ I 1 7 7
I105	FS? 3	▣ ∧ 3 3
I106	XEQ I168	XEQ I 1 6 8
I107	FS? 4	▣ ∧ 3 4
I108	XEQ I157	XEQ I 1 5 7
I109	RCL C	RCL C
I110	RCL D	RCL D
I111	XEQ T051	XEQ T 0 5 1
I112	RCL+ W	RCL + W
I113	STO E	▣ RCL E
I114	x⟨⟩y	x↔y
I115	RCL+ Y	RCL + Y
I116	STO N	▣ RCL N
I117	XEQ I146	XEQ I 1 4 6
I118	VIEW D	▣ R↓ D
I119	VIEW N	▣ R↓ N
I120	VIEW E	▣ R↓ E
I121	RCL E	RCL E
I122	RCL- O	RCL − O
I123	RCL N	RCL N
I124	RCL- U	RCL − U
I125	x⟨⟩y	x↔y
I126	XEQ T062	XEQ T 0 6 2
I127	STO D	▣ RCL D
I128	x⟨⟩y	x↔y
I129	180	1 8 0
I130	+	+
I131	360	3 6 0
I132	RMDR	▣ TAN 3
I133	STO A	▣ RCL A
I134	XEQ I146	XEQ I 1 4 6
I135	VIEW D	▣ R↓ D
I136	CF 6	▣ ∧ 2 6
I137	GTO I001	GTO I 0 0 1
I138	RTN	▣ XEQ
I139	RCL Z	RCL Z
I140	x=0?	▣ MODE 6
I141	AZIMUTH	EQN *Then stroke* RCL *before each alpha input*
I142	FS? 2	▣ ∧ 3 2
I143	XEQ B001	XEQ B 0 0 1
I144	HMS→	▣ 8
I145	RTN	▣ XEQ
I146	FS? 6	▣ ∧ 3 6
I147	VIEW A	▣ R↓ A
I148	FS? 2	▣ ∧ 3 2
I149	RCL A	RCL A
I150	FS? 2	▣ ∧ 3 2
I151	XEQ A004	XEQ A 0 0 4
I152	FS? 2	▣ ∧ 3 2
I153	VIEW B	▣ R↓ B
I154	FS? 2	▣ ∧ 3 2
I155	VIEW Q	▣ R↓ Q
I156	RTN	▣ XEQ
I157	SQ(S)+SQ(D)−SQ(G)	**input as 1 equation** EQN *Then stroke* RCL *before each alpha input*
I158	2×S×D	EQN *Then stroke* RCL *before each alpha input*
I159	÷	÷
I160	ACOS	▣ COS
I161	STO V	▣ RCL V
I162	RCL T	RCL T
I163	RCL- V	RCL − V
I164	STO C	▣ RCL C
I165	→HMS	▣ 8
I166	STO A	▣ RCL A
I167	RTN	▣ XEQ
I168	(S×SIN(V))^2	EQN *Then stroke* RCL *before each alpha input*
I169	STO M	▣ RCL M
I170	SQ(G)	EQN *Then stroke* RCL *before each alpha input*
I171	STO L	▣ RCL L
I172	S×COS(V)	EQN *Then stroke* RCL *before each alpha input*

(Continued on next page)

Program	Keystrokes	Program	Keystrokes
I173 SQRT(L-M)	[EQN] *Then stroke* [RCL] *before each alpha input*	I181 (S×SIN(K))÷ SIN(H)	*input as 1 equation* [EQN] *Then stroke* [RCL] *before each alpha input*
I174 +	[+]		
I175 STO D	[⇄] [RCL] [D]	I182 STO D	[⇄] [RCL] [D]
I176 RTN	[⇦] [XEQ]	I183 RTN	[⇦] [XEQ]
I177 P-T	[EQN] *Then stroke* [RCL] *before each alpha input*	I184 S×SIN(V)	[EQN] *Then stroke* [RCL] *before each alpha input*
I178 STO K	[⇄] [RCL] [K]	I185 STO G	[⇄] [RCL] [G]
I179 180-(K+V)	[EQN] *Then stroke* [RCL] *before each alpha input*	I186 S×COS(V)	[EQN] *Then stroke* [RCL] *before each alpha input*
I180 STO H	[⇄] [RCL] [H]	I187 STO D	[⇄] [RCL] [D]
		I188 RTN	[⇦] [XEQ]

Maintenance (setting/clearing coordinate registers)

The short program to the right, when executed, will set coordinate storage registers one through 150 as coordinate registers. It may also be run whenever you want to clear all of the currently stored coordinates. LN = 42.

You may set a different quantity of registers (instead of 150) by changing the control number at step Z004. For instance, if you use the number 200.01, it will set up 200 registers for coordinate storage.

Program	Keystrokes
Z001 LBL Z	[⇄] [XEQ] [Z]
Z002 [0,0]	[⇄] [( )] [0] [⇦] [0] [0] [ENTER]
Z003 STO K	[⇄] [RCL] [K]
Z004 150.000	[1] [5] [0] [.] [0] [0] [0]
Z005 STO J	[⇄] [RCL] [J]
Z006 RCL K	[RCL] [K]
Z007 STO(J)	[⇄] [RCL] [.]
Z008 DSE J	[⇄] [GTO] [J]
Z009 GTO Z006	[GTO] [Z] [0] [0] [6]
Z010 RTN	[⇦] [XEQ]

Partially clearing Registers

Again, looking at the control number at step Z004, assume that you have 45 or so used coordinate registers and you want to **clear all but numbers 1-15** because they are the basic Control Points for your project that you will be using again tomorrow.

Use the number 150.01501. This means the highest register is 150, you want to stop clearing at 15 (015 because it requires three digits) and you are decrementing by 1 (01 because it requires two digits). The program will now clear only registers above 15 and below 151.

LBL	page	LN	CK*	FLAGS USED								REGISTERS USED																									
				0	1	2	3	4	5	6	10	A	B	C	D	E	F	G	H	I	J	K	L	M	N	O	P	Q	R	S	T	U	V	W	X	Y	Z
A	2	73	B152																																		
B	3	95	EE29																																		
C	3P	1209	3202																																		
D	4, 6	80	1027																																		
E	1P	188	749E																																		
G	6P	1294	D515																																		
H	2P	177	F502																																		
I	11P	786	D599																																		
K	10P	171	9AFC																																		
L	11P	118	4832																																		
P	9P	116	4C5F																																		
S	11P	84	7819																																		
T	9P	246	9536																																		
V	1P	279	6D25																																		
X	34	93	1EBE																																		
Z	14P	42	DC26																																		

*In the earliest release of the HP35s calculators the checksums are not always the same in different calculators. For this book we will give the LN and checksum numbers, but you should *not* rely on the checksums to agree.

If you have the right LN number and the program seems to work, you are probably correct in your input, however you can have the correct LN number and still have an error in a line such as STO A when it should have been STO B. At the time of this THIRD PRINTING we still do not know if the checksum problem has been fixed in the calculators yet.

ISBN: 978-0-944889-49-7

$55.00 U.S.

PREPARATION GUIDE FOR

INVESTIGATING BIOLOGY LABORATORY MANUAL

NINTH EDITION

JUDITH GILES MORGAN
M. ELOISE BROWN CARTER

 Pearson